Euro Noir

Also by Barry Forshaw from Pocket Essentials

Italian Cinema
Nordic Noir

Euro Noir

The Pocket Essential Guide to European Crime Fiction, Film & TV

BARRY FORSHAW

POCKET ESSENTIALS

First published in 2014 by Pocket Essentials,
an imprint of Oldcastle Books Ltd,
P.O.Box 394, Harpenden, Herts, AL5 1XJ
www.pocketessentials.com

Editor: Nick Rennison

A CIP catalogue record for this book is available from the British Library.

ISBN
978-1-84344-245-5 (print)
978-1-84344-246-2 (epub)
978-1-84344-247-9 (kindle)
978-1-84344-248-6 (pdf)

2 4 6 8 10 9 7 5 3 1

Typeset by Avocet Typeset, Somerton, Somerset
in 8.75pt Univers Light
Printed in Great Britain by Clays Ltd, St Ives plc

For more about Crime Fiction go to www.crimetime.co.uk / @crimetime.uk

To all the authors, translators, publishers and filmmakers
who have talked to me during the preparation of this book.

Contents

Introduction

It's not just the Scandinavians. The Anglo-American domination of the crime fiction genre has been under siege by Nordic Noir for quite some time, but another juggernaut is crashing its way into the genre – the astonishingly varied and exciting crime fiction streaming out of other European countries: France, Germany, Italy, Spain, Portugal, Greece and others. Examining and celebrating this exhilarating body of criminal work, I've tried to bring to the continental countries the enthusiasm I've previously shown when writing about Scandinavian crime fiction. From important early writers such as Georges Simenon to more recent giants such as Andrea Camilleri, all the key names (and many new and lively talents) are here in a book I've designed as both guide and shopping list for readers. The initial idea occurred to me a few years ago when I was filming the BBC documentary *Italian Noir* (and its companion, *Nordic Noir*).

But the crime genre is as much about films and TV as it is about books, and *Euro Noir* is as much a celebration of the former as the latter. The hottest new genre on television and the big screen – and the one with the most cultural respectability – is crime film drama from countries other than Britain and America. (*The Sunday Times* has talked about 'a cross-Channel crime wave'.) And with new films and TV shows about to take the phenomenon to ever more stratospheric levels, even more attention will be focused on foreign crime, with its franker, more graphic treatment of violence and sexuality than the Anglo-Saxon version.

First of all, I think it's important to set out the parameters of this book. Let me tell you what *Euro Noir* tries to do – and what it doesn't try to do. The idea is to present a user-friendly, wide-ranging snapshot of the best achievements (both on the printed page and on screen) of crime not originally written (or played) in English. However, unlike my earlier *Nordic Noir* (where even in 160 pages it was possible to present a largely inclusive survey), such comprehensive coverage would obviously be impossible in an area which has been producing splendid work from a variety of countries for so many years and with the space available to me in *Euro Noir*. I've tried to pack in as much as I can. I've concentrated on Western Europe and I've had to be selective, with an emphasis on the contemporary rather than the classic. Even so, you may discover that a favourite of yours is given relatively concise coverage, while someone else may receive what appears to be more generous attention. My rationale was simple. I wanted to present as varied and interesting a picture of the range of foreign crime books and films within the amount of pages available to me, and if some very familiar writers had to be dealt with more concisely in order that new and exciting writers could be given the kind of attention they have not received previously, it was a trade-off I thought worth making. As for the thorny issue of translation: no one is more aware of the inestimable value of that art than I am (as translators who know me will attest!), so I trust I'll be forgiven an occasional inconsistency in crediting these valuable professionals. Four credits I really can't miss, though, are Antonio Hill, Paul Johnston, Quentin Bates and Charles den Tex for their valuable conversations about Spain, Greece, Iceland and the Netherlands respectively.

As for the general issue of which authors and books to include, the pitfalls yawned before me. In the final analysis, I was aware that I was (in any case) on a hiding to nothing. Even when working on a massively inclusive two-volume book such as *British Crime Writing: An Encyclopaedia*, I knew that there were always new writers appearing (often on a weekly basis), along with a host of interesting writers from the past whose work was being exhumed. (The latter is a growing phenomenon these days, particularly with ebook initiatives.) I can only hope that readers will not find the inevitable omissions here too egregious – don't forget that such omissions have at least meant that other, very worthwhile creators have been included.

Holding up the Mirror

Do you consider crime fiction to be a harmless diversion? And do you pack a foreign crime novel when travelling abroad to while away the time on Eurostar? In fact, if you're not paying close attention to the text, you could be missing an incisive and penetrating guide to the socio-economic and political elements of the countries you're visiting, freighted in amidst the detection and rising body count. The ever-growing success of crime fiction (other than the British/American model) is built on the awareness among readers that the best writers from Italy, Germany and elsewhere are now regarded as social commentators with quite as acute a grasp of the way their countries work as any serious journalist. (After the Breivik killings in Norway, who was the pundit most often called upon to talk about the influence of the far right in that country? It was, in fact, Norway's leading crime writer, Jo Nesbo.)

Another corollary of the boom? The popularity of crime in translation may be a modest (but cogent) response to the 'pull-up-the-drawbridge' thinking of Little Englanders. As the translator Kevin Halliwell said to me: 'The extraordinary success of the European crime genre in the UK proves that British readers and viewers are much less insular than some publishers and TV programmers would have us believe. A renewed interest in modern foreign languages – and in translation in particular – is likely to be a serendipitous consequence.'

ITALY

The sun beats down, and cold-hearted murder is done. The very individual (and more laidback) approach to crime fiction in Italy, most Latin of countries – with its endemic political and religious corruption – is fertile territory for crime fiction, not least for the way its deceptive languor is shot through with the ever-present influence of the Mafia.

It is notable (and perhaps regrettable) that, as yet, many of the remarkable and idiosyncratic talents of this Mediterranean branch of the crime fiction genre have not made the mark that their Scandinavian confrères have. But enthusiasm among non-Italian speaking readers is growing. The attentive reader will take on board the sometimes subtle, sometimes direct political insights and historical contexts to be found in the work of such writers as **Leonardo Sciascia**, **Carlo Lucarelli** and (of course) **Andrea Camilleri**. But along with the better-known names, much light may be thrown on the strategies and achievements of writers yet to break through outside Italy. Potential readers, however, should be aware that sheer narrative pleasure is the key element of most Italian crime fiction, rather than (generally speaking) the more astringent sociopolitical fare from other countries. Italy, of course, has produced one of the most ambitious historical crime novels ever written (though one that has defeated many a reader with insufficient patience), **Umberto Eco**'s sprawling, phantasmagorical, philosophical *The Name of the Rose* (1980), a book graced with one of the most celebrated translations ever accorded a non-English language novel, courtesy of William Weaver.

Apart from the Italian writers listed below, mention should also be made of the contribution to the dissemination of Italian crime writing of a man known to many readers as the 'King of the Erotic Thriller'. Due to the burgeoning popularity of the latter genre, his time has certainly arrived and he is now one half of the EL James rival, 'Vina Jackson'. However, crime fiction fans are more likely to celebrate Maxim Jakubowski (born in England to Russian-British and Polish parents and raised in France) as one of the most reliable editors in the field, with a lengthy CV of distinguished entries. One in particular, *Venice Noir* (2012), is part of the long-running 'Noir' series issued by Akashic Books, and is a particularly cherishable entry. The company appears to be working its way through every city on the planet (how long before they get to *Wigan Noir*?), but Italy is solid territory. The writers represented here are an eclectic bunch, with some prestigious Italians (all ably translated) such as the idiosyncratic **Matteo Righetto**, along with some reliable Brits such as Roy Grace's creator, the estimable Peter James. And while we're mentioning Italian crime writers who deserve attention, the following need a namecheck: **Marco Malvadi, Dacia Maraini** (sorely in need of more UK translations), **Giampiero Rigosi**, the more literary **Antonio Tabucchi** and the prolific, highly adroit **Marco Vichi** (whose *Death in Florence* is essential reading).

Latin Temperaments

If French crime fiction lags slightly behind in the social relevance stakes, things are, however, changing in Italy, as that country's crime fiction is gradually coming to terms with a fractured political situation and a long series of political scandals. The doyen of Italian crime writers, **Andrea Camilleri**, rarely engages directly with politics or social issues. (Although, during the massively controversial Silvio Berlusconi era, he did quote Dante: 'The country has the wrong helmsman.'). While his books accept endemic corruption as part of the fabric of Italian society, they are – generally speaking – elegantly written escapist fare. Other writers, such as Carlo Lucarelli and **Giancarlo De Cataldo**, engage more directly with the way society works, but few tackle such issues as bloody-mindedly as recent writers like **Roberto Costantini**.

Andrea Camilleri: The Master

The seal of the best foreign crime writing is as much the stylish prose as it is the unfamiliar settings readers are transported to. When both ingredients are presented with the expertise that is Andrea Camilleri's hallmark, Mr Micawber's words are à propos: result, happiness. Camilleri has familiarised us with his Sicilian copper Salvo Montalbano, a laser-sharp mind, and a gourmet whose mind frequently strays to food. Most of all, we know his stamping ground: the beautiful, sleepy territory of Vigata. And the heat. In *August Heat* (2009), it is omnipresent and crushing.

The novel starts with a sleight of hand, cleverly misdirecting the reader. Montalbano is dragooned into a search for the brattish child of friends. The house they are staying in is thoroughly searched, but there is no place the child could have hidden. Until, that is, Montalbano discovers a hole in the ground that leads to a hidden subterranean floor – one illegally concealed to sidestep planning laws. The child is there, alive, but also in the sunless room is a trunk, containing the plastic-wrapped, naked body of a murdered girl.

All of this is masterfully handled, and will delight Camilleri admirers. But there are caveats. What, for example, of Montalbano's team of coppers? The author assumes we'll know them and offers not a jot of characterisation or description which becomes a problem for new readers. No characterisation, that is, apart from that of Montalbano's clownish assistant, Catarella, long something of a problem for English readers. How do you translate a character who uses broad Sicilian argot? Does a translator – in this instance, the admirable Stephen Sartarelli – render what Catarella says into pidgin English? Or into how pidgin Italian might sound in English? The ungainly compromises here are unsatisfactory ('poisonally', 'he's a one wherats is got a shoe store'), and prompt the thought that perhaps they should be considerably toned down in the translation process. Italian readers may chuckle at the original, but it's a trial for English readers.

But these are minor quibbles, with the customary sardonic rendering of Camilleri's epicurean inspector pleasurable as ever. And the author is always, bracingly, a provocative writer: he has Montalbano admiring (unnamed) the Swedish writers Sjöwall and Wahlöö, and their 'ferocious and justified attack on social democracy and the government'. Such spleen is in Camilleri's novel too, along with the aforementioned thrust at a 'helmsman whom [Italy] would have been better off without'.

More Montalbano

The most striking foreign crime fiction writing may be found in the very personal prose of the best writers as it is in the colourful locales we are taken to. This piquant combination (very much a Camilleri signature) blossoms in *The Wings of the Sphinx* (2009). Here again is Camilleri's intuitive Sicilian copper Montalbano who combines rigorous analytical skills with copiously indulged gourmet tastes. Here again is the pretty, somnolent territory of Vigàta. Montalbano is having problems with his long-distance lover, Livia, and he has other worries: he is aware of the passing of the years and the deadening effect of the violence that is such a constant presence in his job. Then a grisly discovery is made – the corpse of a young woman is found, half of her face missing. The remaining clue to who the dead woman was is a tattoo – the eponymous sphinx. The same mark is to be found on three other young women, Russian immigrants to Italy. All three are sex workers – and all three have disappeared. This is highly involving fare and *The Wings of the Sphinx* (translated by Stephen Sartarelli) is top-notch Camilleri.

In *The Age of Doubt* (2012), an encounter with a mysterious young woman leads Montalbano to the harbour where he is to discover something very strange: the crew of a yacht called the Vanna, which was due to dock in the area, has discovered a body floating in the water. The face of the dead man has been mutilated. Montalbano begins to take a very close interest in the crew of the yacht and its enigmatic owner, the attractive and volatile Livia Giovanni. The most idiomatic foreign crime fiction is a passport to the exotic settings we are transported to, and this element is delivered with the skill that is Andrea Camilleri's stock-in-trade in one of the veteran writer's most recently translated books. We are back in the company of Camilleri's canny Sicilian policeman, whose counterintuitive response to crime remains nonpareil, and his sybaritic gourmet tastes are still firmly in place.

The Track of Sand (2011) will keep admirers more than happy. Montalbano is strolling on the beach near his home when he discovers a dead horse. But when his men arrive on the scene, the horse has disappeared leaving behind only traces in the sand. Later, Rachele, an attractive horsewoman, reports the disappearance of her horse, stabled by one Lo Duca, one of the richest men in Sicily. He, too, has discovered that one of his horses has gone missing. As the above suggests, this is one of the most unusual of Camilleri's novels, and all the winning characteristics we have come to know so well in his epicurean hero are firmly in place.

The Scent of the Night (2005) and *The Potter's Field* (2012) are subtly different from other novels by the veteran writer. In the first, an elderly man holds a distraught secretary at gunpoint, and the doughty Inspector Montalbano finds himself involved. The secretary's employer, a high-flying financial adviser, has disappeared, taking with him several million lire placed in his hands by the citizens of Vigàta. And the case has some personal ramifications for Montalbano, involving building taking place where he doesn't want it to happen – on the site of his favourite olive tree. With the usual quirky characterisation of his epicurean gourmet copper, along with the unflinching insight into the vagaries of human behaviour that are Camilleri's stock in trade, the resulting mix provides one of the most delicious entries in a highly distinctive canon.

In *The Potter's Field*, Vigàta is suffering from storms, among the worse the generally sedate town has known. Montalbano is summoned when a dismembered body is found in a field of clay. The body bears traces of being the victim of an execution, and this would appear – once again – to be the work of the local Mafia. But there are several unanswered questions. Why, for example, was the body cut into 30 separate pieces? Matters are complicated for Montalbano by the strange, uncommunicative behaviour of his colleague Mimi – along with the seductive appeal of Dolores Alfano, looking for Montalbano's help in finding her missing husband. The seal of the best foreign crime writing is as much the stylish prose as it is the unfamiliar settings readers are transported to. When both ingredients are presented with the expertise that is Andrea Camilleri's hallmark, the result is sheer pleasure.

Leonardo Sciascia: The Godfather

The immensely influential Leonardo Sciascia (who was born in Racalmuto, Sicily in 1921 and died in 1989 in Palermo) is one of the most comprehensively significant of Italian writers, celebrated for his swingeing examination of political corruption and the corrosive concomitants of power. His work is shot through with intellectual rigour. Sciascia made his living teaching even when writing and only decided to write full time in 1968. His political commitment was well known: he was a Communist Party representative on Palermo city council, and followed this with a stint working for the Radical Party in the Italian Parliament. From Sciascia's early work in 1950 (*Fables of the Dictatorship* with its critique of fascism) onwards, political engagement was always on the writer's agenda. His first crime-related novel appeared in 1961, the brilliantly written *The Day of the Owl*, with its sharply drawn picture of the Mafia, consolidated in later books. His influence on the many writers who succeeded him is incalculable.

Gianrico Carofiglio: Proust and Prosecution

The elegant Gianrico Carofiglio is very much his own man. Meeting him in the plush fifth floor bar of Waterstone's, Piccadilly, when he was in London to promote his novel *Temporary Perfections* (2011), I was quickly impressed by his erudition (Proust, Chesterton and Steinbeck are cultural reference points namechecked within a few minutes), his fierce intelligence and knowledge of the law (prior to his highly successful crime-writing career, he was celebrated as a prosecutor in the Italian town of Bari), and his extremely proficient English. Yes, Gianrico Carofiglio is his own man – but after just a few minutes in his company it's impossible not to be reminded of another highly successful crime writer.

Carofiglio is tall, attractive and casually dressed in jeans that show just the right amount of distress. His effect on women is quickly evident, and when he talks about the fact that he is regarded by feminine admirers as something of a surrogate for his fictional protagonist, lawyer Guido Guerrieri, it's hard not to think: 'Gianrico Carofiglio is the Italian Lee Child!' And if his hero, Guido, is a more thoughtful, less two-fisted character than the brawling Jack Reacher, he is as much a favourite with female readers as Lee Child's maverick trouble-shooter. Asked about the author/character syndrome, Carofiglio smiles and stretches out his long legs, sinking back into the overstuffed armchair. 'Well, the question I am most often asked by those who read my books is: "Are you Guido?" I used to say no, I'm not; he's a character I write about. But then I realised the effect he was having on readers – particularly women – and I decided to be more... flexible!'

Crime fiction in translation is a taste the English are rapidly acquiring, and writing as vivid and astringent as Carofiglio's should accelerate the trend. The author is a brave man: an anti-Mafia judge in Puglia who has taken on the powerful and (lethal) corruption that is endemic in Italy. His debut novel *Involuntary Witness*, published by plucky independent Bitter Lemon Press in 2010 and followed since by other, well-received books, begins with the discovery of a child's body in a well at a southern Italian beach resort. A Senegalese peddler is arraigned for sexual assault and murder, but Defence Counsel Guido Guerrieri realises that the truth is more complex. A tangled skein of racism and judicial corruption confronts Guerrieri. Italian crime fiction seems more ready to take on uncomfortable social issues than the home-grown product, and

17

Carofiglio's trenchant prose makes for irresistible reading – the latest book, *Temporary Perfections*, is even more accomplished. (His English translators are Howard Curtis and Antony Shugaar.)

His time as a prosecutor has left Carofiglio crammed with the kind of minute legal expertise that he channels so entertainingly (if exhaustively) into his novels, but he is surprisingly dismissive of his time in this high-profile job. 'I suppose I reached something of a midlife crisis,' he says. 'I'd reached the age of 40, and thought "what am I doing?" I realised that I wasn't doing what I wanted to do with my life. Certainly, my job was demanding and fulfilling and it was satisfying to work within the parameters of the law – interrogation, for instance, is a fascinating process (Carofiglio has written popular non-fiction books about the legal profession), but ever since I read Jack London's *White Fang* as a boy, I wanted to write – that book was genuinely life-changing for me. At the age of 40 I decided to buckle down and actually *do* it – to try to write. And to my relief, readers appear to be responding to what I'm doing.'

That, of course, is putting it modestly. Carofiglio's books are highly successful – and almost invariably well reviewed – throughout the world, and he has arrived in London after an exhausting tour of the United States talking about *Temporary Perfections*. His publishers, François von Hurter and Laurence Colchester of Bitter Lemon Press (an imprint that specialises in translated fiction), shake their heads in amazement at just how fresh he looks after his punishing schedule, and how adroitly he deals with all the mechanics of promoting a book – such as this interview.

More coffee is ordered, and I try to draw Carofiglio on the writing process. After Proust and Chesterton as exemplars, he had mentioned how he first read about London in Conan Doyle's fog-shrouded evocation of the city, visible below from Waterstone's fifth floor window. For his writing process, he draws on another literary model. 'Margaret Atwood uses an image that struck me – it's like entering a darkened room and finding a way to the exit. At the exit is – hopefully – the book you have been trying to write.'

He relaxes into a recumbent position. 'The most important thing for me now, though, is writing. When I was a boy I avidly consumed everything: Westerns, films, comic strips, Jules Verne. But like my protagonist Guido I wanted to go after the bad guys. In my time as a public prosecutor, I dealt with everything from Mafia murders to drug trafficking and extortion. Certainly my view of humanity was conditioned by this work – both for good and for ill. And if I can utilise all that in my novels, that's immensely satisfying for me.'

Gianrico Carofiglio possesses *amour propre*, but also something of a quiet modesty, so it is a little surprising when he says: 'After all, I have been described as Italy's best writer of legal thrillers...' And then comes the punchline: 'But then I am Italy's *only* writer of legal thrillers...'

Giulio Leoni and *The Third Heaven Conspiracy*

Fourteenth-century Italy. In an abandoned church on the outskirts of Florence, master craftsman Ambroglio is discovered murdered, having been working on an unfinished mosaic. Yes, *The Third Heaven Conspiracy* (2007) is a historical murder mystery – but who has author Giulio Leoni settled on as his detective to look into this bloody murder? No less than Dante Alighieri, who is to write (after solving this mystery) the immortal *The Divine Comedy*. Here, Dante has been elected to a position of authority – but still finds time to investigate the catacombs (and other dark places) for the killer. An ingenious and atmospheric historical mystery, and one of a growing number of modern novels which reference Dante. (Dan Brown added to this number in 2013 with the phenomenally successful but much-criticised *Inferno*.)

Niccolò Ammaniti

After a lengthy delay, Canongate issued a new paperback edition of Ammaniti's *I'm Not Scared* (originally published in an English translation by Jonathan Hunt in 2003), alongside his later novel *The Crossroads* in 2010. The two books can be read as companion pieces on the complex relationship between father and son, a theme that clearly fascinates Ammaniti – before making his name as a thriller writer, he collaborated with his father (a professor in psychopathology) on an essay on the problems of adolescence entitled 'In the name of the son'.

I'm Not Scared is set in the blisteringly hot summer of 1978. While the adults who live in the few houses that make up Aqua Traverse stay indoors, the children roam the countryside on their bikes. And on one of their excursions, in an abandoned farmhouse, Michele discovers a terrible secret. Ammaniti manages to walk a tightrope between writing from the point of view of the nine-year-old Michele and providing enough information (largely through the voice of the narrator, an older Michele) so that we, the readers, are soon able to connect the fateful discovery with the arrival of a mysterious stranger and the tension pervading the village. Not only is this a gripping, unputdownable thriller, Ammaniti's realistic portrayal of his young hero and Michele's relationship with his friends and family make it a compelling coming-of-age drama.

In *The Crossroads*, the lead character, Cristiano, is slightly older – thirteen. At the centre of the narrative is the complex, loving, but occasionally violent relationship between Cristiano and his father Rino, an alcoholic right-wing extremist who is fighting social services to keep his son. Rino and his two friends – a man who blames himself for the death of his daughter, and a dreamer who was strange even before he electrocuted himself – come up with a plan to solve all their problems: they'll ramraid an ATM machine. But instead of a standard robbery-gone-wrong plot, Ammaniti gives us a series of coincidences and twists that, although totally unbelievable, keep the novel hurtling along. Unlike the earlier *I'm Not Scared*, with its sense of unease and suspense, this is a full-blown black comedy, shocking in its descriptions of violence and human stupidity. The popularity of Ammaniti's books in his native Italy is evidenced by the fact that both these novels have been made into films by Gabriele Salvatores, the director of *Mediterraneo*. His 2011 novel *Che la Festa Cominci* has also been translated into English as *Let the Games Begin*.

Summer with Luigi Guicciardi

In Luigi Guicciardi's intriguing *Inspector Cataldo's Criminal Summer* (2010, translated by Iain Halliday), we are taken to Guiglia – a small Italian resort in the Apennines where nothing much seems to happen. But one hot summer the town's peace is shattered by a series of grisly deaths. Inspector Cataldo is drafted in to investigate the first death, an apparent suicide, and is soon engulfed in a mystery that encompasses events that happened 18 years before, a group of childhood friends, and a stranger who has suddenly appeared in Guiglia. Luigi Guicciardi's protagonist Cataldo is an atypically tall, blond Sicilian, who works methodically and calmly in this, the first in a series of crime novels where the emphasis is very much on solving the puzzle rather than on vivid and unsettling descriptions of violence. Let's hope that the (relatively) new publisher Hersilia Press, the brainchild of Ilaria Meliconi, continues to provide English readers with the further adventures of Inspector Cataldo.

Delivering Evil: Roberto Costantini

Speaking (on several occasions) to Roberto Costantini is something I found a bracing experience; apart from anything else, his cool anatomising of Italian politics is laser-sharp. Before I met him, I was aware that a head of steam had built for his epic novel *The Deliverance of Evil* (2013) – but was it worth all the fuss? The Tripoli-born writer was being touted as an Italian Stieg Larsson, with this first book of a trilogy undergoing a title change in English (the Italian title would translate literally as *You Are Evil*), a troubled central character, a strong and bitter political strain – and even the imprimatur of Larsson's publishers in the UK. But there the resemblances end. In the novel (translated by NS Thomson), Costantini's detective is Commissario Michele Balistreri, and readers patient enough to stick with the unhurried prose will find a picture of an entire society vitiated by corruption along with one of the most fully realised protagonists in modern crime fiction – if, indeed, this can be called a crime novel. In fact, *The Deliverance of Evil* is actually a state-of-the-nation piece, and the failure and stasis of the compromised hero might be read as a metaphor for Italy's untrustworthy authority figures.

The novel is set in two time periods. In Rome in July 1982 (on the eve of the Italian victory at the World Cup in Spain – success or failure at football is a central image), Elisa Sordi, employed by the real estate company of the Vatican, disappears. The investigator is Police Commissioner Balistreri. Self-centred and lazy, he invests little in the case, which ends with the body of a young woman discovered on the banks of the Tiber. The crime remains unsolved, but its repercussions spread out over many years. In July 2006, the dead girl's mother takes her own life, and Balistreri once again becomes involved, but he is now a very different man. Although he has been promoted, crippling remorse plagues him, and his self-loathing is hardly alleviated by antidepressants. The long-buried secrets he is to uncover expose the fault lines in his own troubled society (the background of Costantini's protagonist is keenly drawn, from his devotion to Mussolini and the ultra-right to clandestine work for the security forces as Aldo Moro is murdered by the Red Brigade).

With a new papacy drawing attention to the Vatican, Costantini's novel could not be more timely, though its picture of church power as irredeemably corrupt will not please those hoping for a re-energised Catholic Church (Balistreri himself has been a victim of priestly abuse). *The Deliverance of Evil* is not for the casual reader, but those seeking a substantial, ambitious novel drawn on the most sprawling of canvases will find their commitment amply rewarded.

The Multi-Tasking Giorgio Faletti

I've not yet managed to meet him. I had an event set up at the Italian Institute (and, as usual, I'd done my homework assiduously), but Giorgio Faletti cancelled. Perhaps he'd heard about my Italian, although the event was to be in English! Faletti is a man clearly not content with just one career. Over the years, he has been a lawyer, TV comedian, film actor (e.g. *Cinema Paradiso*) and singer/songwriter – and, what's more, he has enjoyed considerable success in each of these careers. His blockbuster thriller, *I Kill* (2008), had already sold over 5 million copies worldwide before its UK appearance. While most Italian crime fiction is deliberately parochial, Faletti paints his exuberant narrative on the largest of canvases. The template here is very much the grand scale – the international thriller as practised by American and British writers – and he knows exactly what he's doing. The setting is Monte Carlo, playground of the rich and bolthole for the criminal. In *I Kill*, the more upscale residents are being targeted by an implacable serial killer who calls himself 'No One' (shades of Homer's *Odyssey*). A radio talk-show host allows him to announce each killing against a soundtrack that indicates who the next victim will be. And at the scene of each crime are the words 'I Kill' scrawled in the victim's blood. The killer's nemeses are FBI agent Frank Ottobre, struggling to come to terms with the death of his wife, and police Commissioner Nicholas Hulot. Both men have their work cut out for them, as No One continues to cut a bloody swathe through his victims, seemingly unstoppable. Giorgio Faletti is well aware of the imperatives of the international thriller, and presses all the requisite buttons here. The book is long – over 500 pages – but the tension is maintained throughout with genuine skill.

In *The Killer in My Eyes* (2012), Mayor Marsalis undergoes a personal tragedy when his son is found dead in a New York studio, his body stained red and disposed on the floor like Schultz's cartoon character Linus with a blanket by his ear and his thumb in his mouth. Marsalis turns to his brother, ex-policeman Jordan, to look into the bizarre murder. And the killer is to strike again, many times.

Maurizio De Giovanni: The Crocodile

'They've dubbed me the Crocodile, on account of crocodile tears. Brilliant, aren't they? The crocodile cries as it eats its young. But, as you know very well, those aren't my children...'

The Crocodile (2012) by Maurizio De Giovanni is grittily persuasive. Transferred to Naples after a tangle with the Sicilian Mafia, Detective Inspector Giuseppe Lojacono feels that he's marking time, deliberately buried beneath the provincial bureaucracies of the Naples police department while he waits out the ramifications of an awkward scandal. But something begins to stir from beneath the shadowy depths of Naples. The bloodied bodies of teenagers start appearing around the city, victims of a strange and sinister killer whom police and locals take to calling 'The Crocodile', due to the tear-stained tissues he leaves at each and every crime scene. It soon becomes clear to Lojacono that there is a killer out there willing to go to lengths further than he could ever imagine, and that it is only the inspector who can snatch back the city's youth from the jaws of the Crocodile. A bestseller in Italy, *The Crocodile* is a labyrinthine narrative of murder and revenge – and, what's more, a header into the malign psyche of a predator. Maurizio De Giovanni lives and works in Naples. In 2005, he won a writing competition for unpublished authors with a short story set in the 1930s featuring the detective Ricciardi, and then went on to write his bestselling series of Ricciardi novels. *The Crocodile* marks the beginning of a new crime series set in present-day Naples and featuring Detective Inspector Lojacono.

Blood Curse (2013), the second book in the Ricciardi series, develops its protagonist's gift for visions, experiencing vicariously through his own eyes and ears the final seconds in the lives of victims of violent deaths. This gift/curse has helped him become one of the most successful homicide detectives in the Naples police force, but all the horror and suffering has hollowed him out emotionally. He drinks too much and sleeps too little. Other than his loyal partner, Brigadier

Maione, he has no friends. *Blood Curse* is set in Naples, 1931. In a working class apartment in the Sanità neighbourhood an elderly woman has been viciously beaten to death. Commissario Ricciardi and Brigadier Maione arrive and find a wall of silence. Further atmospheric fare from a talented writer, as is *I Will Have Vengeance: The Winter of Commissario Ricciardi* (2012). We are in Naples in March 1931: a bitter wind chills the city's streets, and one of the world's most celebrated tenors, Maestro Vezzi, has been found savagely murdered in his dressing room at Naples' famous San Carlo Theatre. The withdrawn and taciturn Commissario Ricciardi is called in to investigate, and learns that the arrogant, volatile Vezzi had many enemies, and that there are many names in the frame for his killing. Ricciardi, however, has secrets of his own. Anne Milano Appel's intelligent translation does full justice to a richly characterised outing for De Giovanni's aloof copper. An equally atmospheric outing is *Everyone in their Place* (2013), subtitled *The Summer of Commissario Ricciardi*, and cast in traditional vein. The novel is again located in 1930s Naples, with Ricciardi and his colleague Maione making edgy sorties into a world of corrupt aristocrats and extreme right-wing politicians; vintage De Giovanni, in fact.

Michele Giuttari: Hunting Monsters

Is the author Michele Giuttari actually more interesting than his books? Many crime authors are troglodyte creatures who wisely shun the light of day, as their unprepossessing appearances might remind readers how far they are from their charismatic protagonists, but Michele Giuttari (as I found when I met him for an event at the Harrogate crime festival) is almost a stereotypical Latin charmer, handsome in standard middle-aged Italian fashion. More than that, he is the Real Deal in the crime-fighting stakes. A Sicilian-born Inspector of Police, he took on the Cosa Nostra. His elite anti-Mafia squad in Florence investigated the serial killer known as 'the Monster of Florence', who claimed 14 lives, and was an inspiration for Thomas Harris's Hannibal Lecter books. The fact that the killer did not appear to work alone (as Giuttari discovered) uncovered the murky layers of conspiracy that are meat and drink to a crime writer, and Giuttari made the decision to move from police work (where his life had been placed at risk on several occasions) to the more sedate profession of writer. His debut novel, *A Florentine Death* (2007, a massive seller in Italy), is a transmutation of the author's previous life:

Chief Superintendent Michele Ferrara shares his creator's first name, stylish grey-flecked locks and Sicilian turn of phrase (not to mention a German wife). But leaving aside all these antecedents, can Giuttari actually deliver the literary goods? After all, an intimate knowledge of police work doesn't necessarily make a good writer. Inspector Ferrara is investigating a sequence of seemingly random killings: a man is murdered in a shop dealing in religious trinkets, his face mutilated, and a brutal death occurs in an antiques showroom. Ferrara's digging for the truth encounters quite as much bureaucratic interference as any British copper. Indeed, this is a *sine qua non* of the genre, whether the setting is the wet streets of Edinburgh or the sultry piazzas of Florence. And Ferrara, while dealing with a priest who clearly has much to hide, finds himself up against the Calabrian Mafia. All of this is dispatched with a surprising economy and terseness (in Howard Curtis's efficient translation). In fact, the poetic-sounding title is misleading: the writing here is closer to the pared-down style of such Americans as Ed McBain than to Giuseppe Di Lampedusa ('He went in... the body lay on the floor, hidden by the counter. He approached it.') In fact, this tactic (while initially prompting thoughts that the prose could be a touch more nourishing) pays dividends as the novel progresses. The character of Chief Superintendent Ferrara and his associates begin to resonate through this clipped accretion of detail, and the plotting is full of quiet confidence. The air of authenticity (admittedly the one element that could be said to be guaranteed) is persuasive throughout.

After the author parlayed his experience into *A Florentine Death* and *A Death in Tuscany* (2008), his third novel, *The Death of a Mafia Don* (2009), was proof that his new career as a novelist was bearing a rich fruit. A bomb explodes in the heart of Florence, blowing up the car of Chief Superintendent Michele Ferrara of the much-respected *Squadra Mobile*. Ferrara is clearly a target for some very dangerous men, possibly because he has just imprisoned the sinister Mafia *capo* Salvatore Laprua. But then Salvatore Laprua is discovered in his prison cell, dead. 2013 saw the publication of *The Dark Heart of Florence*, another challenging case for Ferrara. Once again, intricate plotting is par for the course as the residents of the city begin to relax after the death of a ruthless serial killer. But then a senator and his butler are found murdered, and Ferrara begins to believe that the case is still open. As so often before, he is to be stymied at every turn by a phalanx of corrupt forces with a variety of vendettas complicating matters even further – not least what appears to be a vendetta against Ferrara himself. All the indications are that he has a powerful nemesis out to bring him down. Is it because of a skein of malfeasance at the very heart of the city? Once again, Giuttari is able to draw upon his own considerable experience of policing in Florence to grant persuasive verisimilitude to his grim and dramatic scenario.

Giuttari's UK publisher, David Shelley of Little, Brown, told me how he'd enjoyed working with the author – and how in general publishing crime in translation has been instructive. 'The satisfactions of publishing European crime writers in the UK in translation are manifold – firstly, I feel I have learnt so much about other countries in doing so: about their police departments, their legal systems, their cultural mores... even down to the food that they eat and the way they spend their leisure time. It is the best sort of armchair travelling one can do! I have also been fortunate enough to work with some superb crime writers and to appreciate both the similarities and differences between the UK and other European countries.

'It is so hard to single any one book or author out, but I would like to highlight two that I have particularly loved. Firstly, I have published the author we've just been talking about, Michele Giuttari's Florence detective series, from the very beginning. We have now published six books in the series and will shortly publish the seventh. I feel very fortunate to work with Michele: he is the highest-ranked member of a police force ever to write crime fiction, and his wealth of experience is fascinating. He is also remarkable at conjuring up the atmosphere of Florence and at building a picture of a city that is at once idyllic but also racked with tensions and which has a dark underbelly to it.

'The other author I would mention is **Donato Carrisi**. His novel *The Whisperer* has been a true international phenomenon and is one of those rare crime novels that works on every level, in every culture. It is non-place-specific but has a storyline that is so enormously compelling that one just has to turn the pages and to recommend it to all one's friends. It has been the archetypal word-of-mouth success for us, selling 100,000 copies just on the back of readers recommending it to each other. Moreover, both Donato and Michele have been truly delightful to work with and have given me a real insight into the world of Italian crime fiction. I feel very lucky to have worked with them both, and to be able to read and publish so many amazing European crime writers.'

Gaetano Savatteri: The Man Who Doesn't Turn

Gaetano Savatteri's *Uomini che non si voltano/Men Who Never Turn Back* (2008) marks him out as a distinguished heir of Leonardo Sciascia. Savatteri writes with candour and insight about crime and Sicilian politics. His third novel is a study of power, a political noir that hinges on the story of three men who were friends at university in Palermo. Years later, fate brings them together again. Placido has become a policeman, but a slander case has led to his suspension; Aurelio is a politician, following the career set out for him by his father, but doesn't have a strong enough character for the cut-throat world of politics; and Silvestre – less defined than the other two, as befitting his chameleon-like character – is a journalist who has ended up working with Aurelio. What brings them together are threatening, anonymous letters received by Aurelio, who calls on Placido to investigate. Regrettably, at the time of writing, this title is not available in English.

The Years of Lead and *Romanzo criminale*

The immense success of **Giancarlo De Cataldo's** novel *Romanzo criminale* (2002), about three close friends who hijack the organised crime scene in Rome, moved into the territory of non-literary phenomenon. The book, complex and heavily peopled, was famously inspired by real-life events. As well as being a compelling crime narrative, it is a chronicle of the 'Years of Lead', the time of socio-political upheaval that extended from the 1960s to the 1980s in Rome, with organised crime and political corruption going hand-in-hand. From a vividly realised 1960, with the joyriding principals already on their way to becoming ruthless criminals, through the bloody battles of the 1970s (including encounters with terrorists, the Mafia and the security services), the period detail is impeccable with the stark and unvarnished presentation of the characters paying dividends in terms of verisimilitude. The current lack of an English translation is inexplicable.

The *Imprimatur* of Monaldi & Sorti

Apparently, the authors Monaldi & Sorti bristle at comparisons of

Imprimatur (2009) to the work of Dan Brown. As well they might: their novel may involve violent death and papal cover-ups, but there the similarity ends. Rita Monaldi's & Francesco Sorti's prose (in Peter Burnett's sympathetic translation) is more subtle than Brown's word-spinning. It seems, however, the husband-and-wife duo is also unhappy about comparisons to a much more prestigious novel: Umberto Eco's *The Name of the Rose*. But here their objections may be a little disingenuous: both books, in fact, are sprawling historical mysteries with a brilliant prelate at the centre of the narrative, and a callow apprentice supplying the Watson figure.

What might grab the attention of English-speaking readers is what the authors (and their publishers) claim is an attempt by the Church to suppress the book. The initial printing was a success, but then the Italian publisher Mondadori decided not to reprint. According to Monaldi & Sorti, there was pressure from the Vatican. The authors claim to have found documents in the secret archives of the Vatican revealing that William of Orange received a sum of money from Pope Innocent XI in Rome. (William was behind the toppling of the Catholic James II from the throne – though the alliance between the Pope and William is not, in fact, a new discovery.) The authors decided to utilise their belief that a Pope had bankrolled a nemesis of the Church as part of a novel, but the timing was unfortunate – as *Imprimatur* was published, the Vatican inaugurated canonisation procedures for Pope Innocent. The couple were, they say, forced to flee Italy (though they now live in Rome). Mondadori (like so much else) is owned by ex-Italian Prime Minister Silvio Berlusconi, and neither Berlusconi nor his publishing house has ever commented on this situation.

Whether we choose to believe all the above or dismiss it as hype, as several commentators have, what does the book have to offer? Atto Melani is a spy at the court of Louis XIV. A local inn is cordoned off after a plague outbreak, and among those quarantined is Melani and his young apprentice, the narrator of the novel. They uncover a plot to assassinate the Pope, the alliance between William of Orange and the Vatican, and a conspiracy to utilise the plague as a devastating weapon against Islam. For the reader who has little interest in ancient papal conspiracies, is *Imprimatur* worth all the fuss? Yes it is, just. This is an exuberant, discursive historical novel. It is certainly not as accomplished as Eco's *The Name of the Rose*, but most readers will find it more accessible, for what that's worth.

Augusto De Angelis: Late 1930s Decadence

Augusto De Angelis is a special case. His protagonist is Commissario De Vincenzi of Milan, whose investigations take place against exotically drawn late Art Deco backgrounds. This historical contextualisation renders the writing more resonant and complex – as do the hidden politics. De Angelis wrote during the years in which Mussolini held power, with an uneasy relationship not dissimilar to that of the composer Richard Strauss and his privately despised fascist masters in Germany. In fact, De Angelis might be said to have inaugurated a literary genre in Italy – the *giallo*. The genre was not taken seriously – except by its dedicated readers. It certainly wasn't by the cultural establishment that regarded the whole field as 'rubbish' beneath consideration. Perhaps suggesting that the relationship between fascist ideals and culture can be identified in his work is a little tendentious (Italian composers such as Ottorino Respighi might be more fruitfully examined here), but the boundaries of freedom of expression are an element in the author's work. A key book is *The Mystery of Cinecittà* (1941) which touches on the sometimes fractious interaction between popular culture and a totalitarian regime, with the very Italian character of his work an innovation. The author had to conform to certain levelling expectations (happy endings, conventional plotting) but sketched in subtle traces of 'anti-fascism', notably in the sceptical, anti-authoritarian persona of the detective. De Angelis's Commissario De Vincenzi books were filmed for Italian television in the 1970s but no current English translations are available.

Crossing the River of Shadows with Valerio Varesi

The rain drives down, the river is threatening to burst its banks. A hulking barge ploughs through the turbulent water, shrouded in fog. Hours later, it runs aground – but the bargeman who set out so hurriedly into the storm is nowhere to be seen. The half-remembered opening chapter of a novel by Dickens? No: the river is not the Thames, but a tributary in the Po valley, and this is a curtain raiser to *River of Shadows* (2010), the first 'Commissario Soneri' mystery by Valerio Varesi. Has the Italian author made himself a hostage to fortune by evoking memories of his heavyweight English predecessor? In fact, Varesi soon proves that he has the measure of his ambitious narrative – a narrative that promises to break the metaphorical banks of an overworked genre. On the same night as the above, the urbane, cigar-smoking Soneri is looking into what appears to be the suicide of a man in Parma, and discovers a link with the missing bargeman – they were brothers. What's more, the Tonna brothers share an ignominious past: they were both militiamen for the fascisti half a century earlier. And Soneri is to find that (as the river recedes) death in the present has fingers that reach back into Italy's benighted past.

Crime writers throughout the world have long cast a cold eye on the political realities of their countries, with several crime novels finding room to excoriate George Bush, for example. (James Lee Burke is one American novelist who has allowed his disdain full rein.) Things are different in Italy, where the controversial prime minister is only now becoming a regular *presenza scura* for such writers as Camilleri. Valerio Varesi is something new: while the corruption at the dark heart of *River of Shadows* springs from the bitter clash of the partisans and the fascists in the past, the author allows echoes of the iniquities of his country's history to resonate in the present.

Some may regret that his protagonist Soneri, though vividly characterised, is cut from a familiar cloth. He's another Italian copper with haute cuisine instincts – fried polenta with wild boar sauce has him salivating – he has problems with authority figures and encounters with sour pathologists, and even laments the semi-obligatory dead wife. But, finally, any reservations about such familiar elements – almost impossible to avoid in the overcrowded ranks of middle-aged coppers – are quickly swept away by the sheer panache of Varesi's prose (particularly when so elegantly rendered in the sympathetic translation by Joseph Farrell). And the real coups of *River of Shadows* are twofold: the author's trenchant analysis of his country's ignoble past married to the narrative acumen of a master storyteller. Readers will be happy to spend more time in the eventful company of Commissario Soneri.

Giorgio Scerbanenco: Malign Milanesi

Giorgio Scerbanenco may be identified as one of the Godfathers of Italian noir. Such books as the sinewy thriller *The Milanese Kill on Saturday* (1969, not currently available in English translation) have congruences with the work of Georges Simenon. There is the same wry attention to provincial life, deception, bad faith and human guilt. The author was born in Kiev (then part of the Russian Empire) in 1911, and moved to Milan at the age of 18. He wrote in a variety of genres, but made his most lasting mark in crime/detective fiction, many of his books being filmed, several of them for TV. His protagonist is Duca Lamberti, a doctor struck off the register for euthanasia, who becomes a detective. His best regarded book – notably literary in style – is *The Milanese Kill on Saturday*, in which Lamberti infiltrates the Milanese underworld, its seedy brothels and violent pimps, in a search for a missing young woman.

Scerbanenco's *Duca and the Milan Murders* features the saturnine, philosophical Lamberti joining his friend, Police Inspector Carrua, in a battle with the murderous criminals of the city. In this novel, Duca becomes involved in a tortuous case of corruption, aided in his investigations by an American girl. The past, as so often, is crucial here: it's necessary to revisit the events of World War II to bring about a resolution. The novel, in its French translation, received the *Grand Prix du Roman Policier* in Paris in 1968. Scerbanenco's *A Private Venus* (1966) is set in the bleak Milan suburb of Metanopoli in the late 1960s. The body of a woman is found by the side of the road. Duca Lamberti has just been released from prison where he has spent three years for having practised euthanasia. He is approached by the rich industrialist Auseri who asks him to cure his son Davide of his drinking habit. After an attempted suicide, Davide explains to Duca how he had met Alberta, the young girl who was found dead a few days earlier, a death for which he feels responsible. A complex web of guilt and betrayal is uncovered with Scerbanenco's characteristic skill.

Hiding from the Mob: The Legacy of *Gomorrah*

The incendiary, lid-blowing book *Gomorrah* (2006) drove its author, **Roberto Saviano**, into hiding, angering his targets by his truthful portrait of the Neapolitan Mafia. The Camorra work with a cocktail of drugs and violence – both utilising and trading in the former. But their activities also extend to the toxic disposal of waste (which, of course, is not actually disposed of at all, but simply dumped) and the procurement of designer goods. This is not to take into account such vicious sidelines as people trafficking. Saviano offers perhaps the most quotidian picture of the day-to-day life and activity of the mob, often crushingly banal, its protagonists stupid and brutal, with the book making no concessions to the romanticising of the subject so often channelled by other writers. Roberto Saviano may have paid a price for his bravery, but his literary legacy is assured with this remarkable document.

Sex, Blood and Barbara Baraldi

Barbara Baraldi's *The Girl with Crystal Eyes* (2010, translated by Judith Forshaw), sets its dark, giallo-influenced narrative in Bologna, painting the city's time-worn network of dark streets (through which a serial killer moves) blood red. A child's discarded teddy bear opens the curtain on a grim investigation conducted by the unrelenting Inspector Marconi and every stratum of the city – high and low – is probed by Baraldi's copper. The murder victims have all had a history of abuse towards women, and all died with erections. Marconi and his associate Tommasi find themselves on the trail of a charismatic woman. The detective encounters a striking red-head (the eponymous 'girl with crystal eyes') who has had a vision of blood – all too prescient, as it turns out.

Barbara Baraldi is something different from her compatriots; she has said that her templates are filmic rather than literary (Dario Argento rather than Andrea Camilleri), with a strong and heady infusion of punk sensibility – and, crucially, a heavy dose of eroticism. Sexuality totally infuses the book, and desire – both male and female – is foregrounded. It's edgy, disturbing stuff and more writing in this vein by Baraldi (along with a host of other Italian writers) can be found in Maxim Jakubowski's compendious anthology, *Venice Noir* (2012) – the scarifying story *Commissario Clelia Vinci*, named after its protagonist.

Not So Dull Days: Massimo Carlotto

'Mediterranean noir is about telling big stories, stories that recount great transformations, stories that denounce what is wrong but at the same time posit the culture of solidarity as an alternative to that of greed and violence,' said Massimo Carlotto, a writer with first-hand experience of the world of crime and the police. A number of crime writers have found inspiration in their everyday lives and experiences, whether on the right or wrong side of the law. But Carlotto has had more real experience of the criminal world than most authors. In Padua, on 20 January 1976, a young girl, Margherita Magello, was repeatedly stabbed and left for dead. A young student radical, the 19-year-old Massimo Carlotto, came to her aid and was covered in her blood. She died, and he was arrested and charged with her murder.

Acquitted and then convicted, he was advised by his lawyer to flee before the sentencing. He went underground in Paris, and then South America, but was betrayed by a lawyer in Mexico. He was tortured following a case of mistaken identity, and then extradited to Italy. Carlotto was imprisoned from 1985 to 1993, when he received a pardon from the President. It is a subject he discussed frankly in the BBC documentary *Italian Noir*, in which the present writer also took part. On his release, Carlotto then wrote the semi-autobiographical novel *The Fugitive* (published in English by Europa Editions in 2007), covering the time (almost 18 years) between his arrest and his pardon.

The precepts he listed in the first paragraph of this section are given their head in Carlotto's *At the End of a Dull Day* (2013, translated from the Italian by Antony Shugaar), and give the book its strength. Giorgio Pellegrini, the hero of Carlotto's *The Goodbye Kiss* (2006), has been on the straight and narrow for years. But that's about to change. His lawyer has been playing him, and now Giorgio is forced into service as an unwilling errand boy for an organised crime syndicate. At one time, Giorgio wouldn't have thought twice about doing whatever was necessary to get out of such a tangled situation, but he now feels he's too long in the tooth to face his enemies head-on. To regain his peaceful life as a successful businessman, he's going to have to find another way to shake off the mob. And though Giorgio's circumstances may have changed, he is still essentially the ruthless killer he used to be.

Patrizia Rinaldi: *Three Imperfect Numbers*

In the elegant translation by Antony Shugaar, Patrizia Rinaldi's *Three Imperfect Numbers* (2013) offers at least one thing markedly different from most other contemporary crime entries in its highly unusual protagonist. The report that has just landed on Commissario Martusciello's desk is unlike any other. The lifeless body of the Neapolitan singer Jerry Vialdi has been found at the Naples football stadium; another body, this time a Jane Doe, has been discovered in the Bentegodi Stadium in Verona, hundreds of miles away. Both bodies were discovered in a foetal position with no obvious signs of physical violence, the method (or madness) behind the deaths unfathomable. A challenge left by a psychopath for the police? Enter Patrizia Rinaldi's ace in the hole: the beautiful superintendent Blanca Occhiuzzi has been blind from birth, and has been forced by the dark that envelops her to perceive the world through only four senses. She intuits the fear in people and feels their guilt and their innocence. It is she who guides her colleague Martusciello by the hand, taking him into the mind of a murderer with her highly attuned senses. It is, in fact, as if he were the blind one. Rinaldi's allusive and unusual writing makes her an intriguing crime author.

Marcello Fois: *The Advocate*

When Marcello Fois's *The Advocate* (2004) was translated into English from Italian by Patrick Creagh, Anglophone readers were suddenly conscious of what a remarkable writer they had missed. The eponymous Advocate is Bustianu, who practises (in an earlier century) in rural Sardinia. A farmworker, Zenobi, is accused of stealing lambs and goes into hiding, even from his counsel. Subsequently a farmer is murdered, and Zenobi is in the frame for the crime. What follows is immensely vivid crime writing with an acute sense of period and locale – but (most of all) characterisation of satisfying colour. There are hints in Fois's writing of the great Leonardo Sciascia, not least in the perfectly judged concision to be found here. (Georges Simenon's not-a-wasted word approach is also, perhaps, in the mix.) What is most striking about *The Advocate* is that, in just a few pages, the reader is aware of just why the work of Marcello Fois is held in such high esteem.

Alessandro Perissinotto: Milanese Menace

An event I chaired in London with Alessandro Perissinotto was notably slowed down by an unnecessary interpreter. His English was fine, although I could not persuade him of this. During the conversation, the author evinced a particular pleasure in his novel *Blood Sisters* (2011, translated by Howard Curtis), and the source of his pride is not hard to discern. The book is a cogent example of Perissinotto's notions about the line dividing criminals from the rest of us which he sees as a nebulous one. The countryside around Milan is wrapped in crepuscular darkness as psychologist Anna Pavesi digs in the icy soil, looking for... what? Just over a week earlier, Anna has been approached by the well-heeled Benedetta Vitali with a request to investigate the circumstances surrounding the death in a road accident of her half-sister Patrizia and the subsequent disappearance of the latter's body. Anna is not a detective, there has been a misunderstanding, but she is short of money and agrees to take on the assignment. It will lead her into a labyrinth of false clues and wilful deception in which appearances are deceptive. Was Patrizia's death merely a commonplace hit-and-run incident on a country lane, or was there something more sinister behind it?

Fascist Memories:
Carlo Lucarelli's Commissario De Luca Trilogy

While working on his thesis on the history of law enforcement during the Fascist period in Italy, Carlo Lucarelli interviewed a man who had been an officer in the Italian police force for forty years. He had started as a member of the Fascist political police but, towards the end of World War II, when the Fascists were on the run, he answered to partisan formations then in control of the country. His job? To investigate the Fascist hierarchy, his former employers. After the war, when regular elections were held and a government formed, he was employed by the Italian Republic. Part of his job was again to investigate and arrest his former employers, this time the partisans. Carlo Lucarelli, however, never finished his doctoral thesis. Instead, Commissario De Luca was born, and overnight his creator became one of Italy's most acclaimed crime authors. The De Luca trilogy (in splendid translations by Michael Reynolds) begins with *Carte Blanche* (2006), set in April 1945, the final frenetic days of the Salò Republic. A brutal murder on the good side of town lands Commissario De Luca in the middle of a hornet's nest where the rich and powerful mix drugs, sex, money, and murder. This was followed by *The Damned Season* (2007) in which De Luca is on the run under an assumed identity to avoid reprisals for the role he played during the Fascist dictatorship. Blackmailed by a member of the partisan police, De Luca is obliged to investigate a series of murders, becoming a reluctant player in Italy's post-war power struggle. The final novel, *Via delle Oche* (2008), won the Scerbanenco Prize. The time is 1948, with the country's fate soon to be decided in bitterly contested national elections. A corpse surfaces in a brothel at the heart of Bologna's red light district, and De Luca finds himself unwilling to look the other way when evidence in the murder points to prominent local power brokers. The novels (whose tone often veers alarmingly between the sardonic and the massively cynical) are built around one key thesis: the deforming effect of Italy's compromised, slippery politics on every individual, not least the pragmatic but beleaguered De Luca.

The Italian Crime Screen

The Italian crime film blossomed after the constraints of the anodyne cinema of the Fascist era were removed, and post-war developments in both arthouse movies and popular crime fiction began to leave their marks on the genre. Neorealism, peopled at times with frank representations of criminals, prostitutes and black marketers, left a mark that can be seen in such films as Alberto Lattuada's sinewy and compelling The Bandit (1946), along with celebrated art cinema fare such as Bitter Rice (1949, directed by Giuseppe De Santis), which synthesised the unvarnished, realistic elements of neorealism with crime ingredients. With such components derived from popular crime literature (notably the use of violence to resolve conflict), a variety of uncategorisable films appeared. In the 1940s, such films as Pietro Germi's bleak Lost Youth (1947) borrowed from American Noir, and in 1950, the confident Germi laid personal claim to making 'the first Italian crime film.' It wasn't, of course, but the film was significant in being a strange version of one of the central texts of modern Italian literature. The Facts of Murder (1959) was a very free version of Carlo Emilio Gadda's radical and experimental novel That Awful Mess on the Via Merulana (1957). The director juxtaposes two apparently contrasting genres – police drama and comedy, and Germi himself, perhaps ill-advisedly, took on the role of a police inspector. It was maybe this division of his labour (and attention) which led to a diffuse, fitfully successful adaptation. Other iconic, socially committed Italian films like Pasolini's Accatone (1962) and Rosi's classic gangster film made the same year, Salvatore Giuliano, deserve mention, as do the best of the gruesome giallo crime films of the 1970s and the fast-moving police procedurals (the brutal poliziotteschi) that followed them.

By the 1960s, neorealist filmmakers incorporated socio-political concerns into their work while using crime accoutrements, notably the talented Francesco Rosi and Carlo Lizzani. The latter forged two striking film biographies of ruthless criminals with *Wake Up and Kill* (1966) and the much-lauded *Bandits in Milan* (1968) with both directed in cool, non-emotional fashion. Casting here was iconic: the charismatic Gian Maria Volonté demonstrated his expertise in impersonating hard-edged villains, a specialty that he was to refine frequently over the succeeding years. The next decade brought Elio Petri's memorable *Investigation of a Citizen Above Suspicion* (1970) and a new and influential genre, the violent and kinetic *poliziotteschi*. The genre began as a series of crude simulacra of American models (as so often in the magpie culture of Italian popular cinema), but parlayed the elements borrowed from such US models as Don Siegel's *Dirty Harry* and William Friedkin's *The French Connection* into something different, sometimes injecting indirect social criticism into their borrowed raiment. Italian actors such as Franco Nero were employed, but past-their-best American stars were also used. In non-Italian territories, *poliziotteschi* were only available in crudely English-dubbed versions, which did such films as Sergio Martino's *The Violent Professionals* (1973) no favours whatsoever. One director, Fernando Di Leo, managed to incorporate a personal vision (and a frenetic hand-held camera) into a quartet of lively *poliziotteschi*, the first two based on the writings of Giorgio Scerbanenco, *Calibre 9/Milano calibro 9* (1972) and *The Italian Connection* (1972, with Mario Adorf prefiguring Joe Pesci's terrifying violence in *Goodfellas*), while *The Boss* (1973) and *Rulers of the City* (1976) are snapshots of the 1970s 'years of lead' in which church, state and criminal hierarchies are inextricably intertwined.

TV Omertà

Once the subject of a silencing Omertà, Sicilian gangsters were to be seen on Italian TV in recent years; and large viewing figures were recorded for series such as the multi-episode version of *Romanzo criminale* (differing markedly from the successful film), but of Italian TV crime the most successful export has been the long-running *Inspector Montalbano*, presenting a more roseate view of the country.

Murder and the Giallo

Even taking into account the Western as refracted through the Latin imaginations of Leone and co., the Italian horror film was probably the finest flower of the country's popular cinema, but of equal long-term significance are the stylish murder thrillers known as *gialli*. The most adroit exponents in the latter field (apart from the groundbreaking Riccardo Freda) were Mario Bava, Dario Argento, Sergio Martino and the less talented Lucio Fulci. Once a despised genre (principally because of the crass dubbing to which they were invariably subjected), *gialli* have undergone a major critical re-assessment, with their visual stylishness and bizarre plotting now celebrated. These grisly whodunits, inspired by the yellow-jacketed thriller 1930s/40s paperbacks that enjoyed immense success among Italian readers, utilise certain strategies. With their high-gloss surfaces (widescreen and colour are almost always *de rigueur* for the genre), the essential paradigms were a sumptuously photographed series of murder set-pieces in upscale apartments (the victims usually beautifully dressed, sensuous women), apparently committed by a sex-obsessed psychopath. The murder weapon is customarily a knife, brandished in a black-gloved hand. But this twisted psychopathology motive is almost invariably a red herring: mammon is usually at the centre of the killings, with greed and financial gain being the leitmotif as the source of the bloodletting. (The *reductio ad absurdum* of this schematic is Bava's *Ecologia del delitto/A Bay of Blood* [1971], where the treatment of the murder motivation is almost absurdly casual.)

So what sort of work populated the genre? The film that might be considered one of the first *gialli*, Mario Bava's *Sei Donne per L'assassino/Blood and Black Lace* (1964), is comfortably the director's most influential film on the cinema of other countries – and a key work in the field, with narrative and visual tropes that instantly became templates for the glossy catalogues of mayhem in the films of Argento and others.

However, directors whose names have acquired very little cachet over the years produced provocative work in the genre, such as Paolo Cavara, whose *La tarantola dal ventre nero/The Black Belly of the Tarantula* (1971) has gleaned a certain reputation (which may be partly due to the fact that it was unseeable for several years). Regrettably, however, while flashes of inspiration are to be found, it is a fairly workaday effort, with occasional moments of imagination illuminating the grim proceedings. The method of the killings is notable: a similar technique to that by which certain wasps paralyse tarantulas before eviscerating them. Erotic elements are foregrounded here quite as much as any violence, with a nude Barbara Bouchet undergoing a sensuous massage before she is bloodily slaughtered.

Eccentricity (of a self-conscious variety) is a hallmark of the genre. *La casa dalle finestre che ridono/The House with the Laughing Windows* (1976), directed by Pupi Avati, sports another outlandish title, and in this case is a suitably outlandish film to match. Avati engineers an ingenious (if absurd) narrative that functions intriguingly in its own right, rather than being a way of stitching together a variety of bloody setpieces. In 1950s Italy, a painter accepts an invitation to repair a fresco in a local church. The artist originally responsible for the piece enjoys a poor opinion in the town, and his fresco shows Saint Sebastian undergoing torture. Right from its opening sequence (in which a bloody stabbing is repeated seemingly *ad infinitum*), this is another piece firmly aimed at the exploitation market. But that is not to say that Avati is not capable of the visual invention of more ambitious films.

There is a fascinating – and phoney – internationalism to the *giallo*. The pseudonymous credits attempting to fool Italian audiences into thinking they were not watching a low-prestige local product were one tactic; another deception extended to the use of foreign locations: some cursory pickup shots in a foreign city would be intercut with sumptuous interiors shot in a Rome studio. When *gialli* choose London as their setting, the results are often very odd indeed. In *Gli occhi freddi della paura/The Cold Eyes of Fear*, directed by Enzo G Castellari in 1971, the off-kilter London scenes add another stratum of delirium to the generally odd proceedings.

Bizarrely poetic titles are another fingerprint of the genre, as with *Passi di danza su una lama di rasoio/Death Carries a Cane* (1972), directed by Maurizio Pradeaux. The Italian title of the film translates as 'Dance Steps on the Edge of a Razor', which is actually a better title than the one that its English and American producers chose to go with. (The movie itself, in this case, is entertainingly grotesque, with performances pitched at nigh-operatic levels.)

But how relevant to *giallo* credibility are *auteur* credentials for the director? Luciano Ercoli's *Le foto proibite di una signora per bene/The Forbidden Photos of a Lady Above Suspicion* (1970) demonstrates that second-rank directors could make substantial contributions to the *giallo* genre. A perfectly calculated genre exercise with minimal inspiration from its journeyman helmsman, it's also an exemplar of an attitude to female sexuality typical of the genre, with its fetishistic and menacing games with a knife. In the *giallo* field, of course, fetishistic imagery is the order of the day, and those looking for a more enlightened, feminist view of female sexuality should look elsewhere. (In fact, it would probably be a good idea for such individuals to ignore the *giallo* genre altogether.) But for those prepared to take the controversial fare on offer without being offended, the feast of violently unsettling and erotic imagery frequently has a charge that Baudelaire and Poe would have applauded.

For all their delirious visual invention, plotting is not the strong suit of the *giallo* – what mostly serves for plotting is a tortuous stitching together of disparate narrative elements to provide integument for the blood-drenched set pieces. But the same charge might be levelled at the masterpieces of Hitchcock, except that the English director was canny enough to hire the best screenwriters to provide such texture along with psychological verisimilitude – another element only fitfully present in most *gialli*. If such quality writing is in shorter supply in the Italian films, the exuberant staging, sanguinary inventiveness and constant visual flourishes provide more than sufficient frissons.

Selected Films and TV (by date)

Ossessione (Film, 1942, Luchino Visconti, director)
Of the multiple film versions of James M. Cain's saga of adultery and murder *The Postman Always Rings Twice*, this remains one of the most intense and erotic (despite the graphic and sweaty couplings on the kitchen table in the Jack Nicholson/Jessica Lange/Bob Rafelson version), though it is probably the most joyless in its treatment of Cain's key theme. It's certainly more direct in its treatment of the unbuttoned sexuality of the novel than the John Garfield/Lana Turner/Tay Garnett version, constrained as that was by the draconian censorship of 1940s Hollywood. But Visconti's transposition of the narrative from depression-era America to provincial Italy allows him to comment on the stunted life the protagonists lead. The film – the director's debut – was, in fact, the first to be labelled 'neorealist'.

The Facts of Murder (Film, 1959, Pietro Germi, director)

Perhaps the best approach to this slightly eccentric film version of Gadda's *That Awful Mess on the Via Merulana* is to forget the original novel (with its Joycean experimentations in language and structure) and enjoy the film on its own terms. While it may not function as a model example of literary adaptation, *The Facts of Murder* still boasts many intelligent touches, and is infused with a genuine cinematic sensibility. Events in the narrative are propelled by a masked burglar stealing from the apartment of Commendatore Anzaloni, leading to the introduction of an eccentric *dramatis personae*.

Mafioso (Film, 1962, Alberto Lattuada, director)

The larger-than-life actor Alberto Sordi is perhaps best-known for his work with such directors as Federico Fellini but, in *Mafioso*, he demonstrates his range. Sordi is an amiable factory supervisor who has been residing in Milan with his wife from the North. He returns to his native Sicily only to find that nothing has changed there – and that an oath he made many years before will come back to haunt him, forcing him into behaviour that he will find abhorrent. In the twenty-first century (not least with the television series *Montalbano*), non-Italian audiences have become used to the differences in way of life, language and so much else between Sicily and the North, but Lattuada's intelligent film is an early treatment of the theme made at a time when the word 'Mafia' was hardly to be heard in American films. (The euphemistic phrase 'The Organisation' was most often used instead.)

Salvatore Giuliano (Film, 1962, Francesco Rosi, director)

By no means a straightforward gangster film, *Salvatore Giuliano* is both an examination of the life of the 28-year-old criminal discovered shot to death in a Sicilian courtyard and a cool disquisition on the nature of truth and perception – both historically and in the context of film itself. Rosi's film is an early example of post-modern consciousness in its interrogation of the nature of its own presentation. Essentially, the film is a document detailing the career of the ambitious gangster (who was also a Sicilian separatist), his associates and the mystery of who exactly killed him, but the director also takes on board the interaction between the movement for independence, the Mafia and the local police, while examining social conditions in post-war Sicily. The fragmented infrastructure demands close attention on the part of the viewer – which it repays.

The Violent Four/Bandits in Milan (Banditi a Milano) (Film, 1968, Carlo Lizzani, director)

The final robbery committed by the 'Banda Cavallero' (which was followed by their famous escape through the streets of Milan in 1967) is treated in a nigh-documentary style by Carlo Lizzani, somehow managing to infuse the action sequences with the exhilaration of typical Hollywood product while still retaining a measured sociopolitical tone. Once again, Gian Maria Volonté etches a truly memorable portrayal of malignity as the self-regarding criminal Pietro Cavallero.

Investigation of a Citizen Above Suspicion (Film, 1970, Elio Petri, director)

Perhaps influenced by Albert Camus's The Outsider in its cool refusal to make easy judgement, Elio Petri's stylish and impressive film sets out its facts, shrewdly allowing the audience to change their minds about the characters during the course of the narrative. The chief of detectives in the Homicide division murders his mistress and provocatively plants clues pointing to his own responsibility – but he finds it harder to assume his guilt than he might have considered. The film may be read as a document about Italy's collusion with evil in the Second World War and the subsequent antiseptic treatment of national guilt.

The Bird with the Crystal Plumage (Film, 1970, Dario Argento, director)

Despite sorely testing the good will of his admirers with a recent series of misfires, the key director of the modern giallo is the talented Dario Argento. In his earlier films, Argento's visual and aural assaults on the sensibilities of the viewer put the emphasis on the total experience of film rather than intellectual appreciation of a well-crafted script. Argento's 1970 feature film debut, the poetically titled The Bird with the Crystal Plumage, augured well for his career. A commercial success in its day, it now comes across as a fascinating dry run for many ideas to be more fully developed in later films. There are visual delights galore – a marvellously Hitchcockian chase of a yellow-jacketed hired killer (one of several loose ends not really tied up) that ends with a joke worthy of North by Northwest, a murder by razor that utilises sound as chillingly as Polanski did in Repulsion. The film, though, remains a tyro effort, however dazzling.

The Conformist (Film, 1970, Bernardo Bertolucci, director)

One of Bernardo Bertolucci's most impressive films, with remarkable contributions from Jean-Louis Trintignant and Stefania Sandrelli. Bertolucci's anti-hero is a repressed homosexual who shot a man who attempted to molest him when he was a child. He decides to enter into a loveless marriage, and agrees to act for the Fascist party. His assignment is to kill his ex-professor. The synthesis of politics and Freudian psychology is fastidiously maintained, and the two female stars in particular (Sandrelli and Dominique Sanda) offer memorable performances.

The Case of the Scorpion's Tail (Film, 1970, Sergio Martino, director)

Despite the inconsistency of Sergio Martino's career as a director, the Spanish-Italian co-production *The Case of the Scorpion's Tail* is unquestionably one of his most assured and confident pieces, with the clichés of the crime genre playfully inverted or given a novel twist by a director enjoying the fact that he is so completely in charge of his material. (Martino has admitted that Henri-Georges Clouzot's film of the Pierre Boileau/Thomas Narcejac novel *Les diaboliques* was a template for his work – as it was for Hammer Studios' earlier series of black and white psycho thrillers.) Beneath the seductive surface of the movie (with its kinetic, blood-boltered set pieces, Hitchcockian flourishes and perfectly judged widescreen *mise-en-scène*), the plot, as so often with such movies, is absurd and bears little scrutiny. As so often in the genre, human venality is the plot engine here, but there are piquantly novel touches, such as the double helping of vicious murderers to match the duo of toothsome heroines.

The Mattei Case (Film, 1972, Francesco Rosi, director)

Of Francesco Rosi's various treatments of the lives of real-life gangsters and criminals, *The Mattei Case* is perhaps the most dispassionate, detailing with a cold-eyed gaze the life of the mafia boss who eliminates a slew of rivals to assume pole position. He is, of course, ultimately no luckier than the director's other subjects of criminal biography. Rosi does not judge, but his Manichean universe is unrelenting.

Casa d'appuntamento/The French Sex Murders (Film, 1972, Ferdinando Merighi, director)

This bizarre and frequently maladroit concoction has to be seen to be believed (and, in its unlikely way, enjoyed... sort of). Basically an extremely grisly police procedural, this Italo/German co-production sports a gallery of international stars (including an overweight Anita Ekberg) falling prey to a brutal murderer in set pieces clearly inspired by the delirious *gialli* of Mario Bava. But what makes this so unusual is the inspector assigned to the case: professional Bogey lookalike, the inexpressive Robert Sacchi. With his dyed black hair and trench coat, he doggedly pursues a psychotic killer in a characterisation that is entirely a variety turn. Other than the Bogart mannerisms, 'Inspector Fontane' is a blank – and what's a tough 1940s Yank doing in charge of a 1970s French police force? For connoisseurs of the outrageous, this is... collectable.

Lucky Luciano (Film, 1973, Francesco Rosi, director)

Another one of Francesco Rosi's mesmeric and unemphatic studies of major criminals, shot in typically judicious fashion and rigorously avoiding melodrama. Luciano (Gian Maria Volonté on chilling form) plays a major Mafia capo, elbow-deep in bloodshed and betrayal. The notion that power corrupts has rarely been given such a thorough workout.

The Vigilante (Film, 1974, Enzo G. Castellari, director)

Standard fare for the *poliziotteschi* genre, but dispatched with an infusion of crude exuberance that renders it always watchable, if almost totally lacking in nuance. Notably absent, also, is any kind of social commentary, even of a generalised nature, but Castellari (rarely more than a journeyman genre director) is less interested in such things than he is in producing a tightly edited, tough thriller. Genre stalwart Franco Nero knew just what was required here, and scales down his performance accordingly.

Rabid Dogs (Film, 1974, Mario Bava, director)

While often overblown and repetitive, *Rabid Dogs* (with its air of a young man's guerrilla filmmaking) represents an astonishing change of pace for its then-ageing director. Mario Bava was noted for his carefully controlled, studio-shot Gothic exercises. So different is this late film (with its violent criminals and hostages in a car) that it is hard to believe he is the director. Nevertheless, this very personal low-budget film renders its hostage situation both claustrophobic and tense – and apart from anything else, it allows the viewer to speculate on what kind of a career Bava might have had, had he chosen the crime film rather than the horror film as his *métier*.

The Big Racket (Film, 1976, Enzo G. Castellari, director)

Enzo Castellari grabs his violent and uncomplicated material with both hands and dispatches it with gusto, even managing (in the Italian version at least) to suggest the schism between cynical urban Italy and the Arcadian life in smaller villages. (The crass English dub, as ever, largely obliterates such subtleties.) Fabio Testi's dogged cop takes on the thugs who have a small Italian village in thrall, utilising violence and extortion. When a restaurant owner is brave enough to defy the criminals by reporting to the Testi character, he pays a heavy price: his young daughter is raped. As so often in such fare, the bloody-minded, rule-breaking protagonist enjoys no cooperation from his superiors, who are constantly telling him to stop his investigation. All ends in an explosion of bloodshed. This is one of several *poliziotteschi* that enjoyed a wide currency outside its native Italy.

Illustrious Corpses (Film, 1976, Francesco Rosi, director)

Certain directors (such as Rosi) were always aware that the way to utilise the iconic actor Lino Ventura was... iconically. In *Illustrious Corpses*, Ventura is on typically scabrous form as the relentless Detective Inspector Rogas, commissioned to look into the unexplained murders of several Supreme Court judges. Rosi also draws powerful support from Tino Carraro, Marcel Bozzuffi and Paolo Bonacelli.

Death Dealers (Film, 1976, Umberto Lenzi, director)

The director of *Death Dealers*, Umberto Lenzi, is best known for unflinching, in-your-face exploitation fare such as *Man from Deep River* (1981) and the gut-munching cannibal epic, *Eaten Alive!* (1980), but he has also dabbled in the Italian crime genre with the lively *Rome Armed to the Teeth* (1976). His most assured work in the genre is this tightly-directed effort with its *Bullitt*-inspired car action. The reliable actor Maurizio Merli does most of the heavy lifting here (as he did in 1975's *Violent Rome* and *Rome Armed to the Teeth*). In order to boost US and UK marquee value, the American actors John Saxon and Barry Sullivan are shoehorned into the narrative, prolonging their in-eclipse careers at some distance from their earlier work with Marlon Brando and Barbara Stanwyck.

Inspector Montalbano (TV, 1999–, various directors)

The different (but positive) response of British viewers to the beautifully shot TV series *Montalbano* from that they gave to bleaker Nordic drama was perhaps predicated on the degree of reality that audiences mentally accorded the show. While viewers were prepared to accept the unforgiving urban landscapes of Scandinavian film and crime fiction as realistic, they appeared to look upon the Italian crime drama series, based on the much-loved novels by Andrea Camilleri, in more indulgent, hedonistic fashion. They savoured the warm glow imparted by the Mediterranean setting, the blue skies, a personable Latin hero tackling none-too gritty crimes – all of which were provided by this glossily made series, in which the town of Vigàta, with its unspoilt, antique beauty (unmarred by even a scribble of graffiti), provided a sumptuous wish-we-there backdrop. With the canny casting of Luca Zingaretti in the title role, the series carefully laundered out the provocative elements that occasionally surface in Camilleri's original novels.

However, adaptations of *The Snack Thief*, *The Voice of the Violin*, *The Shape of Water* and *The Terracotta Dog* do economical justice to the original books, and it is a pleasure for us to share the gracious life of the Italian copper. His life is stressed, but alleviated by private lunches at his favourite restaurant and trysts with his on-off girlfriend, Livia, played by Katharina Böhm. The series is always watchable, if rarely challenging, and gave birth to a prequel in 2013, addressing the cases of a younger Montalbano. Montalbano has a way of finding a clandestine relationship between a host of crimes. These involve dirty doings within the Sicilian Mafia (usually on the periphery) and respectable business institutions. But while the characterisation here is as adroit as one could wish, it's plotting that remains the *chef d'oeuvre* of Montalbano. So popular is the series in Italy that Camilleri's home town changed its name to that in his books – Vigàta.

Romanzo criminale (Film/TV series, 2005, Michele Placido et al, directors)

It was inevitable that Giancarlo De Cataldo's novel about three young criminals in Rome would lead to a film adaptation (and subsequently an over-extended TV series), but the material (in the case of the latter) was a victim of its own success, with the dramatic possibilities entering a repetitive, cyclical mode. The refusal to make any of the self-serving, violent characters sympathetic (or in possession of even minimal moral or humane qualities) is already to some extent overextended in the successful film. There it matters less but it becomes a major problem in the TV series. In the case of, say, De Palma's *Scarface*, we are happy to see a monstrous, overindulging – but charismatic – character bring about his own destruction, and engaging our sympathy is not really relevant. But, in the course of the *Romanzo criminale* TV series, although it is efficiently made, the problem assumes paramount importance, particularly as we are soon in the 'one-damn-thing-after-another' syndrome, in which bad behaviour by the brutal and ruthless protagonists is repeated *ad infinitum* and *ad nauseam*. Nevertheless, both film and TV series are made with considerable skill and acted with an unshowy truthfulness that largely keeps such reservations at bay.

Gomorrah (Film, 2008, Matteo Garrone, director)

This caustic, unromanticised vision of Italy's modern-day crime families is distinguished by naturalistic performances from such actors as Gianfelice Imparato, Salvatore Abruzzese and Toni Servillo. Matteo Garrone's multi-stranded film is now regarded as the definitive vision of the all-powerful Neapolitan crime network, the Camorra, and is similarly recognised as an unvarnished picture of the everyday machinations of the Mafia; the film gleaned a slew of awards. Garrone is wise to retain the uncompromising characteristics that made Roberto Saviano's source book something of a phenomenon (and which, of course, led to a variety of death threats to the author, and a life in hiding). *Gomorrah* eschews linear structure to present a piecemeal approach to the lives (and sometimes violent fates) of the characters, and grants total plausibility to the often gruesome narrative. Garonne paints his bleak picture on the most ambitious of canvases, with frequent shots of the masses of ordinary residents, their lives – in large or small ways – in thrall to an all-pervasive criminal organisation.

Salvo (film, 2013, Fabio Grassadonia & Antonio Piazza, directors)

Winner of the 2013 Grand Prix prize at Cannes, *Salvo* (at a stroke) joins the ranks of intriguing Italian mafia thrillers, skilfully handled by two of the most ground-breaking and up-and-coming directors in European cinema, showcasing a strong central performance from Saleh Bakri. The film also signals further indication of an invigorated Italian cinema, as demonstrated by the likes of *Gomorrah*, *I Am Love*, and Sorrentino's 2013 box-office success *The Great Beauty*. A henchman for the Sicilian Mafia, Salvo is solitary, cold and ruthless. When he sneaks into a house to eliminate someone from a rival Mafia clan, he discovers Rita, a young blind girl who powerlessly stands by while her brother is assassinated. When Salvo decides to spare her life, something extraordinary happens. From then on, the two – both victims of the world to which they belong – are linked together.

Young Montalbano (TV, 2013–, various directors)

Montalbano returns, rejuvenated and recast in *Young Montalbano*. Following the massive success of *Inspector Montalbano*, the volatile Italian policeman returned to TV screens at the start of his career, with all the integrity intact, but less of the experience of his older, wiser self. Starring Michele Riondino in the title role, the programme is set in the early 1990s and gives an insight into the private life and early crime-fighting career of the idiosyncratic Sicilian detective. The prequel series was popular in Italy and debuted on BBC Four in 2013. Exhausted by the never-ending hillsides of his rural Sicilian beat, the Deputy Inspector is in the middle of investigating a murder when he finds himself promoted to Inspector and dispatched to his childhood home of Vigàta. There he is called upon to take control of the local police station and gradually build his team with both Fazio Senior and Fazio Junior, Domenico 'Mimi' Augello and the clownish Officer Catarella. Production values and production here are a match for the Zingaretti episodes, but if there is a caveat (apart from the continuing unreality of the policing on display), it is that the dynamic of the later series is established too quickly, with little chance for organic growth. The fractious relationship between Montalbano and idiotic comic relief Catarella, for example, is in place by the second episode, as are – similarly precipitately – several other elements of the original show.

FRANCE

Crime à la Français

In the early twenty-first century, French crime fiction is in good shape – as it was a century ago. An iconic figure in French crime fiction from an earlier era is elegant thief Arsène Lupin, who featured in a series of novels (20 in all) by Maurice Leblanc. These were followed by Lupin stories by other hands and a slew of film and stage adaptations. Leblanc (1864–1941) rivalled even Conan Doyle in popularity, a popularity maintained with the appearance of five sequels from the pen of the writing duo of Pierre Boileau and Thomas Narcejac (discussed separately). Lupin first appeared in short stories in the magazine *Je sais tout*, beginning in 1905. He is a Gallic cousin of E W Hornung's Raffles, whose illegal actions are designed not to alienate the reader – sometimes by the tactic of making his nemeses more criminal than he is. However, from the first major crime author in translation – the influential, prolific and (as he told us) priapic Georges Simenon – to eccentric modern talents such as Fred Vargas, the history of crime fiction from France has been both striking and unorthodox. And, despite earlier Gallic precursors, the creator of Inspector Jules Maigret (and the most important French writer of crime fiction) surely deserves primary consideration. But, before considering Simenon, it's necessary to look at one of his illustrious predecessors.

The Onlie Begetter: Zola

Two lovers who can't keep their hands off each other's bodies and who have sex on the floor; an inconvenient and unattractive husband who needs to be removed. I know what you're thinking: James M Cain's *The Postman Always Rings Twice*. Or one of its many imitators? No, another writer got their earlier... No less than Emile Zola, with his carnal and

49

unsparing *Thérèse Raquin* in 1867. Who can write about sex like Zola these days, with everyone now flinching in advance of ironic but ultimately censorious awards or political correctness? Such as this timeless passage:

Then, in a single violent motion, Laurent stooped and caught the young woman against his chest. He thrust her head back, crushing her lips against his own. She made a fierce, passionate gesture of revolt, and then, all of a sudden, she surrendered herself, sliding to the floor, on to the tiles. Not a word passed between them. The act was silent and brutal.

Reading the 2013 Vintage Classics translation by Adam Thorpe of *Thérèse Raquin* (a tie-in with a new film version of the novel) is salutary. It makes one realise for the first time why Zola was so shocking in his day. Actually, Vintage have done this before. There was a radical new translation the publisher commissioned of Dostoyevsky's *The Devils* (as *Demons*) in the late 90s. Crime writers looking to re-energise their batteries when writing about murder and sex might profitably pick up a novel which was written a hundred and fifty years ago and learn from a master, though both books demonstrate a disgust for sensuality born of crime which would do the sternest Catholic moralist proud.

Georges Simenon: My Friend Maigret

Crime in translation may be achieving massive breakthroughs in the twenty-first century but, long before this trend, one writer was a standard bearer for the field. Georges Joseph Christian Simenon was born in Liège on 13 February 1903 (despite being Belgian, he's placed in the French section of this book because of his iconic French detective and settings); his father worked for an insurance company as a clerk, and his health was not good. Simenon found (like Charles Dickens in England before him) that he was obliged to work off his father's debts. The young man had to give up the studies he was enjoying, and toiled in a variety of dispiriting jobs including, briefly, working in a bakery. A spell in a bookshop was more congenial, as Simenon was already attracted to books, and his first experience of writing was as a local journalist for the *Gazette de Liège*. It was here that he perfected the economical use of language that was to be a mainstay of his writing style, and Simenon never forgot the lessons he acquired in concision. Even before he was out of his teenage years, Simenon had published an apprentice novel, and became a leading light of an enthusiastic organisation styling themselves 'The Cask' (La Caque). This motley group of vaguely artistic types included aspiring artists and writers (along with assorted hangers-on). A certain nihilistic approach to life was the philosophy of the group, and the transgressive pleasures of alcohol, drugs and sex were actively encouraged, with winding-down periods in which these issues (and, of course, the arts) were hotly debated. All of this offered a new excitement for the young writer after his sober teenage years. Simenon had always been attracted to women (and continued to be enthusiastically so throughout his life) and in the early 1920s he married Règine Renchon, an aspiring young artist from his own home town. The marriage, however, was not to last.

Despite the bohemian delights of the Cask group, it was of course inevitable that Simenon would travel to Paris, which he did in 1922, making a career as a journeyman writer. He published many novels and stories under a great variety of *noms de plume*.

Simenon took to the artistic life of Paris like the proverbial duck to water, submerging himself in all the many artistic delights (at a time when the city was at a cultural peak, attracting émigré writers and artists from all over the world), and the writer showed a particular predilection for the popular arts. He became a friend of the celebrated American dancer Josephine Baker after seeing her many times in her well-known showcase *La revue nègre*. Baker was particularly famous for dancing topless, and this chimed in with the note of sensuality that was to run through the writer's life. But as well as sampling the fleshpots (along with more cerebral pursuits), Simenon became an inveterate traveller, and in the late 1920s made many journeys on the canals of France and Europe. There was an element of real-life adventure in Simenon's life at this time, when he became an object of attention for the police while in Odessa (where he had made a study of the poor). His notes from this time produced one of his most striking novels, *Les gens d'en face* (1933), which was bitterly critical of what he saw as the corrupt Soviet regime. As the 1930s progressed, Simenon wrote several of the police procedural novels featuring doughty Inspector Maigret (his principal legacy to the literary world), but he did not neglect his world travels, considering that the more experience of other countries he accrued, the better a writer he would become.

Sentence of Death

Like many Frenchmen, Simenon's life was to change as the war years approached. In the late 1930s, he became Commissioner for Belgian refugees at La Rochelle, and when France fell to the Germans, the writer travelled to Fontenay. His wartime experiences have always been a subject of controversy. Under the occupation, he added a new string to his bow when a group of films was produced (under the Nazis) based on his writings. It was, perhaps, inevitable that he would later be branded a collaborator, and this stain was to stay with him for the rest of his career. After the war, he decided to relocate to Canada, with a subsequent move to Arizona. The United States had become his home when he began a relationship with Denyse Ouimet, and his affair with this vivacious French-Canadian was to be highly significant for him, inspiring the novel *Trois chambres à Manhattan* (*Three Rooms in Manhattan*, 1946). The couple married, and Simenon moved yet again, this time to Connecticut. This was a particularly productive period for him as a writer, and he created several works set in America, notably the powerful *The Hitchhiker* in 1955. With its scabrous picture of the destructive relationship between a husband and wife, this echoed the tough pulp fiction of James M Cain. He also tackled organised crime in *The Brothers Rico* of 1954 (subsequently filmed). Towards the end of the 1940s, Simenon became convinced that he was going to die when a doctor made an incorrect diagnosis based on an x-ray. The novel *Pedigree* (1948) was written under this erroneous sentence of death, but Simenon's time was not yet up. However, always attracted by the prospect of a new relationship, Simenon began to neglect his wife and started an affair with a servant, Teresa Sburelin, with whom he set up house (Denyse ended her days in a psychiatric institution).

By 1971, it had become clear that Simenon was the most successful writer of crime fiction (in a language other than English) in the entire genre, and his character Maigret had become as much of an institution as the author. Simenon created something of a stir with his autobiography in 1971, *Quand j'étais vieux* (*When I was Old*), in which he made his controversial claim that he had had sexual relations with over 20,000 women. This astonishing assertion was met with both scepticism (how had he managed to be such a prolific author if his entire time seems to have been spent in libidinous pursuits?) and a certain distaste at what seemed like boastfulness.

But, leaving such things aside, by the time of his death in 1989, it was clear that the author had created a writing legacy quite as substantial as many more 'serious' French literary figures. And Simenon now seems like the Trojan horse for the explosion of interest in foreign crime writing that has taken place in both England and America.

The Simenon novels that can be described as stand-alones (i.e. books in which no continuing detective figure features) are among the most powerful in the genre. But there is absolutely no debate as to which of his creations is most fondly remembered: the pipe-smoking, heavyset French Inspector of Police, Jules Maigret. The detective first appeared in the 1930 novel *Pietr-le-Letton* (*The Case of Peter the Lett*, or *Pietr the Latvian*, as it's called in a new Penguin translation by David Bellos), and the author has stated that he used characteristics that he had observed in his own great-grandfather. Almost immediately, all the elements that made the character so beloved were quickly polished by the author. Commissaire in the Paris police headquarters at the Quai des Orfèvres, Maigret is a much more human figure than such great analytical detectives as Conan Doyle's Sherlock Holmes, and his approach to solving crimes is usually more dogged and painstaking than the inspired theatrics of other literary detectives. What Simenon introduced that was new in the field of detective fiction was to make his protagonist a quietly-spoken observer of human nature, who focuses the techniques of psychology on the various individuals he encounters (both the guilty and the innocent). Interestingly, Simenon also gave his protagonist an almost ecclesiastical function, in which his job is to actually make people's lives better (although this usually involves the tracking down and punishing of a clever and devious criminal). To highlight this concept of doing some good in society, Simenon decided that Maigret had initially wished to become a doctor, but could not afford the necessary payments to achieve this goal. He also had Maigret working (early in his career) in the vice squad, but with little of the moral disapproval that was the establishment view of prostitution at the time. (Madame de Gaulle famously sought – in vain – to have all the brothels in Paris closed down.) Maigret, with his eternal sympathy for the victim, saw these women in that light and remained sympathetic, even in the face of dislike and distrust from the girls themselves (in *Maigret and the Hotel Majestic*, 1942, the detective has to deal with a prostitute who meets his attempts at understanding with a violent physical attack).

Épater le Bourgeois

Whereas modern coppers such as Ian Rankin's Inspector Rebus are rebellious mavericks, eternally at odds with their superiors and battling such indulgences as alcoholism, Maigret is a classic example of the French bourgeoisie, ensconced in a contented relationship with his wife. There is no alcoholism, but rather an appreciation of fine wines – and, of course, a cancer-defying relationship with a pipe (the sizeable pipe collection on his desk rivals Holmes' violin as a well-known detective accoutrement). André Gide famously described Simenon as 'the greatest French novelist of our times'. Hyperbole, perhaps, but as a picture of French society, the Maigret books (such as *My Friend Maigret*, 1949) collectively create a fascinating panoply. There's social criticism in here as well – Maigret is always searching for the reasons behind crime, and sympathy is as much one of his qualities as his determination to see justice done.

Simenon inspired many writers of psychological crime, such as Patricia Highsmith (as she once told me at a publisher's launch party in London – Simenon's name caused her to brighten up in a way that my mention of Hitchcock's film of her first book, *Strangers on a Train*, had not). Simenon's life was deliberately enshrouded in mystery. Behind the closed doors of one room in his Swiss château, he would surround himself with fetishes. Entering an almost trancelike state, he would write compulsively, usually completing an entire book in five, nine or eleven days. His early thrillers featured psychological portrayals of loneliness, guilt and innocence that were at once acute and unsettling. *The Strangers in the House* (1940) depicts a Simenonian recluse, whose isolation is shattered by the discovery, one night, of a dead man in his house. The subsequent investigation will draw this former lawyer back into humanity, to take the case of the murder himself. *The Man Who Watched the Trains Go By* (1938) shows a man who is very much involved in society, a respectable family man, until the shipping firm, for which he is managing clerk, collapses just before Christmas. A barrier in Popinga's mind falls and there emerges a calculating paranoiac, capable of random acts of violence, capable even of murder. As he feels himself drawn to Paris on Christmas Eve he enters into a disturbing game of cat and mouse with the law. Rushing towards his own extinction he is determined to be recognised, for the world to appreciate his criminal genius. In 2013, Penguin began an ambitious programme to issue all 75 Maigret novels in new translations.

Boileau & Narcejac: Les diaboliques

Their influence on crime novels and cinema has been prodigious – so why isn't the critical stock of Boileau & Narcejac higher? When Alfred

Hitchcock saw the effect on audiences of Henri-Georges Clouzot's *Les diaboliques/The Fiends* (1955), he realised that this Hitchcockian French film – with its superb orchestration of suspense (including horror in a bathroom) and twist-filled plotting of immense ingenuity – would have been absolutely perfect material for him, and subsequently proceeded to make a film using very similar tactics, *Psycho* (1960). In the original novel of *Les diaboliques*, Ravinel has drowned his wife Mireille in her bath, and, aided by his mistress Lucienne, he has dropped her body into a river to suggest suicide. But as Mireille is dead, how is she able to correspond with him from beyond the grave? (Details were tweaked for Clouzot's film.) Regrettably, the plot for *Les diaboliques* has subsequently been borrowed so often, it is now over-familiar.

The prolific and ingenious French writing duo, Pierre Boileau and Thomas Narcejac, who had produced the original novel on which Clouzot's film was based, had written another deviously plotted book, *D'entre les morts/From Among the Dead/The Living and the Dead* (1954), and it was this book that provided the basis for one of Hitchcock's supreme pre-*Psycho* masterpieces, *Vertigo* (1958). This was recently voted the best film of all time in a poll of *Sight & Sound* magazine critics, and while one might demur from that judgement, it's a welcome turnaround from the unenthusiastic critical response it initially received. The importance of the duo – principally through the films influenced by their work, notably a long-running series of psychological thrillers from Britain's Hammer studios – continues to this day. But this immensely professional team of Gallic scribes was not only responsible for much inventive crime fiction but wrote intelligent critical essays on the genre, along with a number of children's stories. (While prowling *les bouqinistes* alongside the Seine years ago, I picked up, in some excitement, several books by the authors, only to find when I returned to London that they were the duo's 'juveniles'. They were capably enough written, but, frankly, I was looking for something as good – and as adult – as *Les diaboliques*.)

Boileau was born in Paris in 1906 in the 9th Arrondissement, and became a voracious consumer of American crime fiction as well as such eventful serials as *Fantomas*. His first detective novel was *Deux hommes sur une piste* published in 1932, inaugurating a lengthy career, only interrupted by wartime service when he was a prisoner of war. Thomas Narcejac (a *nom de plume*; his real name was Pierre Ayraud) was born in 1908 at Rochefort-sur-Mer, and his literary influences included *Arsène Lupin* (the discovery of the crime novel in 1916 was accompanied by the loss of an eye from an accident with a gun). He inaugurated his writing career for the series *Le masque* in 1946.

The team's first collaboration, *L'ombre et la proie*, appeared in instalments from 1951 to 1952, producing a series of joint efforts which appeared every year for several decades. Some of these pieces were spins on their beloved Arsène Lupin.

Voyeurism and Obsession

Perhaps their most celebrated collaboration came in 1952 with *Les diaboliques*, filmed two years later by Henri-Georges Clouzot without the team's input: the corpse of a murdered wife vanishes only to make a shock reappearance. Clouzot's film switched the sex of the victim and murderer, and inaugurated a lengthy series of sleight-of-hand murder plots along similar lines. (In fact, it's comfortably the most channelled plot in crime fiction and films, although perhaps 'the most ripped-off' plot might be a less charitable but more on-the-nose description.) Two years later, the novel *From Among the Dead/Cold Sweat* was filmed as *Vertigo* by Hitchcock, but the director famously revealed Boileau & Narcejac's major plot twists halfway through the film, stating that he was more interested in the psychology of voyeurism and obsession than in merely deceiving the audience who, he calculated, would – in the context of a film – guess the novel's carefully concealed dénouement.

A further eight novels by the duo received film or television treatment, and the writers were responsible for some remarkable screenplays themselves, such as Franju's celebrated (and poetic) *Les yeux sans visage/Eyes without a Face* in 1959 and, a year later, the same director's *Pleins feux sur l'assassin*. Their own expertise in the mechanics of thriller writing was matched by an impressive scholarship regarding the genre. Both men were acute critics of crime novels. But the question remains: why has their star faded in recent years? Perhaps it is the fact that the machine-tooled plotting was sometimes foregrounded at the expense of characterisation. The latter was always functional rather than organic – and the many imitations have retrospectively cast over their own work a perception that they themselves are mechanical in their manipulations of narrative. But many a less accomplished writer has held the stage longer. It is perhaps time for a reappraisal of the extensive oeuvre of Boileau & Narcejac, including such economical thrillers as *The Victims* (1965) and *The Evil Eye* (1959).

Armand Cabasson and Claude Izner: Two who are Three

France has produced some *nonpareil* writers of historical crime fiction. Two of them are actually *three* excellent writers. Armand Cabasson has written several highly accomplished detective novels set during the Napoleonic Wars ('The Napoleon Murders'), which have sold over a hundred thousand copies in France. One example is *The Officer's Prey* (2007), which has the now-familiar device of a protagonist with modern sensibilities freighted into the meticulously observed period setting. In June 1812, Napoleon begins his invasion of Russia leading the largest army Europe has ever seen. But amongst the troops of the Grande Armée is a savage murderer whose bloodlust is not satisfied in battle. When an innocent Polish woman is brutally stabbed, Captain Quentin Margont of the 84th regiment is put in charge of a secret investigation to unmask the perpetrator. Armed with the sole fact that the killer is an officer, Margont knows that he faces a near-impossible task and the greatest challenge of his military career.

'Claude Izner', the author of the best-selling *Murder on the Eiffel Tower* (also 2007) is actually the pseudonym of two sisters, Laurence Lefèvre and Liliane Korb. Their detective is Victor Legris, who is a bookseller. They have both been booksellers themselves on the banks of the Seine, one on the right bank, one on the left bank. I group them together neatly here not just because of the congruences in their work, but because I chaired a lively event with the trio in London's other Parisian *quartier*, South Kensington (where English is occasionally spoken), at the Institut Français. All three shared a very dry Gallic humour, particularly the two sisters, who make a lively double act.

The Izner duo's *Murder on the Eiffel Tower* is (as with the work of the highly individual Fred Vargas) an example of excellent French crime writing by a female writer (in this case, of course, two women) masquerading under a male moniker. The brand-new Eiffel Tower is the glory of the 1889 Universal Exposition. But one sunny afternoon a woman collapses and dies on this great Paris landmark. Can a bee-sting really be the cause of death? Or is there a more sinister explanation? Enter young bookseller Victor Legris. Present on the Tower at the time of the incident, he is determined to find out what actually happened. In this colourful evocation of late-nineteenth century Paris, the reader follows Victor as his investigation takes him all over the city, the deaths begin to multiply and he is caught in a race against time. *The Père Lachaise Mystery*, another quirky example of their work, is set a year later in the Paris of 1890. Lady's maid Denise le Louarn fears the worst when her mistress, Odette de Valois, vanishes from the Pere-Lachaise cemetery during a visit to her husband's grave. Alone in the great metropolis Denise knows just one person she can go to for help: Odette's former lover, Victor Legris, When the frightened girl turns up at his bookshop and tells him her story, Victor feels there must be a simple explanation for the disappearance. But as he begins to look into the matter, it soon becomes clear that something sinister lies behind events at the PeÃre-Lachaise. Gallic, a now-established publisher specialising in translated crime, made the book available in the UK and this elegantly written, ingeniously plotted novel launched the imprint with real élan. France has produced a matchless crime-writing duo before in Boileau and Narcejac – the two women who are Claude Izner are among their honourable successors.

Dominique Manotti:
Rough Trade and Dead Horsemeat

Dominique Manotti was born in Paris in 1942. *Rough Trade* (2002), her first novel, was selected as 'Best Thriller of the Year' by the French Crime Writers' Association and was chosen Book of the Year in the *Independent* by Amanda Hopkinson and Joan Smith, while *Dead Horsemeat* was shortlisted for the Duncan Lawrie International Dagger Award 2006. Manotti's particular skill is to weave an authoritatively plotted crime story with a sharp evocation of the northern landscape that is her territory; gritty urban low-life, too, is a specialist area. *Rough Trade* drew comparisons with American novelists such as James Ellroy, but Manotti's grasp of social issues, economics and malign political influence is more sophisticated than most US practitioners – perhaps David Simon's TV series *The Wire* (particularly the episodes written by George Pelecanos) is a better reference point here.

A favourite book of Manotti aficionados is *Affairs of State* (2009, successfully filmed, see film section), translated from the French by Amanda Hopkinson and Ros Schwartz. The novel is an uncompromising saga of betrayal and corruption. A prostitute (whose incendiary black book contains her upscale international clientele) is found murdered in an underground garage; a plane bound for Iran laden with illegal arms disappears from the skies over Turkey; and the president's closest adviser, Bornard, head of a controversial Elysée security unit, manipulates the system with consummate ease and disregard for issues of legality. Rookie investigator Noria Ghozali determines to untangle the threads which bind these events together. In doing so, she penetrates the Elysée's innermost system, confronts the workings of money and corruption within government, and in the process is forced to combat the institutional – and overt – racism which repeatedly stalls her.

Hopkinson and Schwartz had earlier translated *Dead Horsemeat* (2006), an inside account of horse-racing and drug-trafficking, political shenanigans, public corruption and the durability of human decency. As the May '68 generation comes of age, ideals turn into business deals, deals which spread across the new network of a Europe without frontiers. School friends who campaigned together at Rennes in the heyday of 1968, Agathe Renourd and her protégé Nicolas Berger are in charge of the communications network of a major insurance consortium; Christian Deluc has become a council member at the Elysée Palace; Amelie raises thoroughbreds. Now, in 1989, the paths of these former students are due to cross in an entirely unexpected fashion as they start playing with fire, carried along by the euphoria born of power. Racehorses die under mysterious circumstances, unimaginable quantities of cocaine appear at Parisian parties and dashing Nicolas Berger meets a violent death when a bomb explodes in his car. All the elements that distinguish Manotti's best work are firmly in place, as they are in *Lorraine Connection* (2008). Set in the fictional town of Pondage, Lorraine, the subject here is complex industrial double-dealing. The Korean Daewoo group manufactures cathode ray tubes. Working conditions are abysmal, but as it's the only source of employment in this bleak former iron and steel-manufacturing region, the workers daren't protest. Until a strike breaks out, and there's a fire at the factory. But is it an accident? The Pondage factory is at the centre of a strategic battle being played out in Paris, Brussels and Asia for the takeover of the ailing state-owned electronics giant Thomson. Unexpectedly, the Matra-Daewoo alliance wins the bid. Rival contender Alcatel believes there's foul play involved and brings in the big guns led by its head of security, former deputy head of the national security service. Intrepid private cop Charles Montoya is called to Lorraine to investigate, and explosive revelations follow – murder, dirty tricks and blackmail. Manotti resists the temptation to over-egg the pudding, keeping all the diverse elements of her narrative in perfect balance, and incorporating any elements of social commentary in unforced fashion.

Georges-Marc Benamou: The Ghost of Munich

Certain books (such as *The Ghost of Munich*) arrive with an element of presold success. The novel was an unrealised film project for the Czech director Milos Foreman (responsible for *Amadeus*), from a screenplay by ex-president Vaclav Havel. But Georges-Marc Benamou hardly needed these prestigious (if non-delivering) midwives for the film of his book; he already moved in rarefied circles. Benamou's biography of François Mitterrand created a furore in France (the author was an intimate of the late President). And Benamou became a favoured member of the inner circle of Nicolas Sarkozy, who hired him as cultural adviser. But all these impressive societal connections would count for little if he had not been able to deliver the goods as a writer, and *The Ghost of Munich* was proof that he could cannily combine the 'high concept' novel with a talent for historical fiction. The central character is, in fact, a forgotten man. The theme of the book is the betrayal of Czechoslovakia at the Munich conference in 1938. The destiny of nations was sealed at a meeting between Hitler, Mussolini and the British PM Neville Chamberlain. This was, of course, the occasion after which Chamberlain produced the piece of paper guaranteeing 'peace with honour' – an ignominy he was never to live down, as Hitler, contemptuous of those he had duped, began to cut a bloody swathe through Europe.

But another leader was present at that monumental betrayal – a man many people outside France would be hard-pressed to name. He was the French Prime Minister Edouard Daladier, who returned to his country with the same illusory promise of peace that Chamberlain trumpeted. He is the eponymous Ghost of Munich – and the choice of him as protagonist (rather than the more famous participants) is a masterstroke. The notion of putting one of history's nowhere men at the centre of one of the great tragedies of the twentieth century pays dividends, as Benamou contrasts the weak and vacillating nature of his antihero with the overbearing egos of those with whom he is supposedly sealing a historic pact. Daladier, on his return to Paris, was hailed as a hero – the man who had removed the threat of another war with Germany. But Daladier's tragedy (in Benamou's measured narrative) is his lacerating knowledge that he has failed – and that his failure is one of catastrophic proportions. Shaun Whiteside's translation does deft justice to the text, but he is unable to do much with Benamou's occasional tendency to freight chunks of history into his narrative in a rather artificial fashion. Daladier tells himself things that he already knows, for the reader's benefit. But this does not detract from the steady trajectory of the novel, with its scarifying portraits of Hitler and Mussolini.

Claudie Gallay: The Breakers

In a Normandy village, a woman is coming to terms with the disappointments of her life, spending her days cataloguing migratory birds. A stranger appears at the local bar asking a series of difficult questions – and makes their clear that he is not prepared to leave until he receives answers. His enquiries relate to the local lighthouse and its keeper. But the village sets up a hostile wall of silence. Gallay's atmospheric and highly individual novel continues the tradition of provocative and unusual fiction that is the hallmark of the publisher MacLehose Press, a specialist in fiction in languages other than English. The translation from the French by Alison Anderson is subtle and allusive, as befits the text.

The Phantasmagorical Paris of Jean-François Parot

Perhaps the centuries-old enmity between Britain and France is over. Certainly, a literary *entente cordiale* is in place in Jean-François Parot's novel. Early in *The Phantom of Rue Royale* (set in eighteenth-century Paris) it's clear that the writer exerting a not-so-subtle influence on the text is English rather than French. There are references to the 'best' and 'worst' (of Parisians, not times), and someone is knocked down by a dangerously driven carriage and left to bleed on the ground ('from inside the carriage, an arrogant voice gave the order to push the rabble aside and carry on'). But these signs that we might be in for a reworking of

Dickens's *A Tale of Two Cities* from a Gallic perspective are misleading, though Parot certainly shares Dickens's taste for an operatically staged set piece. And the set piece that opens this outing for Parot's highly intelligent Commissioner Nicolas Le Floch is a doozy, setting a kinetic pace for the narrative that is rigorously maintained. It is May 1770, and the whole of Paris is in a frenzy of anticipation: the Dauphin has married Marie-Antoinette, and the city authorities have laid on a spectacular firework display. But as the youthful Commissioner observes the excitement, he realises that the preparations for the event are wholly inadequate. The fireworks display is mismanaged, and wreaths of black smoke and flame engulf the pyrotechnicians' platform; the crowd panics and the Rue Royale and the Tuileries are plunged into chaos, with people crushed by the carriages and the crowds. However, there is one body among the dead that appears not to be a victim of the disaster, but of a cold-blooded murderer. Nicolas is determined to track down her killer – even though his boss has handed him a more dangerous assignment: find out who is behind the débacle of the wedding celebrations that ended in death. As in such earlier books as *The Châtelet Apprentice*, Parot demonstrates that he has few peers at marrying a colourful historical narrative with the exigencies of the crime novel. The translation by Howard Curtis does full justice to the assiduously detailed prose, and at the centre of things, Nicolas Le Floch is an engaging guide for the reader through the teeming and phantasmagoric capital city that is Paris in the eighteenth century. Perhaps a little pruning might have been applied to that besetting sin of historical fiction, characters needlessly telling each other things they already know ('Pont du Corps-de-Garde, which leads to the Tuileries Gardens, is closed'), and a supernatural element may be a genre-shift too far for some – but such is the momentum of the storytelling here that not too many readers are likely to be worried by this.

Fred Vargas: Don't trust the name

Sitting in a French restaurant a few years ago with one of the most celebrated of Gallic crime writers – after the smoking ban was introduced – made me realise that the forthright Fred Vargas is not a woman who accepts rules without demur. She kept determinedly taking out her Gauloises, making her publisher, agent and the maître d' visibly nervous. But she'd put them away again. For a while. But who is Fred Vargas?

First of all: don't trust the name. As the above makes clear, Vargas, one of the most acclaimed of all current European crime novelists (though her idiosyncratic work is not to every taste), may have a male moniker but she is a woman. Vargas trained as an archaeologist, and she adopted the latter half of her pseudonym in homage to the seductress played by Ava Gardner in *The Barefoot Contessa*. Fred is really Frédérique; she's a dab hand at the accordion, loathes travel (hence the largely Parisian settings of her books), and has made it clear that she'd run a mile before getting mixed up in a real crime case. So why is she so highly thought of? And why are her books selling to more than just aficionados of European crime writing? Her celebrity began in modest fashion: published in France by a small publisher, she can now boast sales of 220,000 (that's the number of copies her riveting novel *Have Mercy on Us All* achieved).

The Three Evangelists firmly demonstrates why Fred is spoken of in such warm terms. Her books have a very individual tone of voice – Gallic, but universal in their cutting psychology, and the personalities of her characters are rendered with off-kilter skill. In *The Three Evangelists*, Greek opera diva Sophia Siméonidis finds that a tree has mysteriously appeared in her Paris garden. She enlists the aid of her neighbours to crack the mystery, and they're just the people to help her: disgraced copper Vandoosler and the down-at-heel historians who are the eponymous Three Evangelists – Marc, Lucien and Mathieu. Tempted by both the mystery and the money on offer, they investigate – but come up with nothing. Then their opera singer neighbour vanishes – and her body turns up as a charred pile of ashes in a car. The quartet now has a murder to solve – and a variety of suspects, including the singer's lover, niece and husband.

A Vargas novel is as good as a trip to Paris. The style has the same hyper-real quality as all her writing – the real world, but filtered through a strange prism – but it's the plotting that really hits the spot: ingenious and eccentric. There was a brouhaha when the Crime Writers' Association decided to exclude novels not written in English from its prestigious Dagger award with the consolation of a separate prize for foreign writers. But after reading Fred Vargas, you may feel that she deserves the main trophy.

There are those who find Vargas's highly unorthodox detective stories just too outrageously plotted, but aficionados know that this is her special ability: she invariably creates narratives that resemble absolutely nothing else in the genre and her novels are all the better for that. *Wash This Blood Clean from My Hand*, another example of her peculiarly European crime writing, starts with an unusual premise. Between 1943 and 2003, nine people have been stabbed to death with a curious weapon: a trident. While all the murderers had been (apparently) brought to justice, there is one bizarre detail: each lost consciousness on the night of the crime and has absolutely no knowledge of their act. Commissaire Adamsberg (whose colleague is the sceptical Danglard) has decided to look into this long-running mystery, and has settled on the imposing judge Fulgence as his prime suspect. Soon, of course, history is repeating itself. This is Vargas's weightiest and most ambitious tome, but shot through with that nervy and sardonic Gallic humour that is her métier.

Eccentric Skills

Similarly, *The Chalk Circle Man* once again firmly demonstrates why she is spoken of in such warm terms. Her books have a very individual tone of voice – Gallic, playful and witty, with the personalities of her characters conjured up with eccentric skill. Here, her canny copper Adamsberg is investigating strange blue chalk circles appearing on the streets of Paris. Another Vargas title well worth investigating is the caustic *This Night's Foul Work*.

I have found discussions with the writer and academic David Platten of Leeds University useful in understanding Vargas's work. He has remarked on the fey aspects of the writer in his book *Pleasures of Crime: Reading Modern French Crime Fiction* (New York/Amsterdam: Rodopi, 2011):

'Vargas is intrigued by popular folklore... the myth of the werewolf and... the history of vampirism. These are worlds in which objects may come to life, or at least acquire significance that extends beyond that of their material existence. Generally it will be because they hold a crucial position in the plot of the given novel, but their magical qualities also allude to the survival into twenty-first-century Europe of the old beliefs which persist in our superstitions and widespread fascination with the supernatural. The implication [is] that the mythological structures developed by our ancient ancestors have somehow percolated through our DNA, resulting in the more or less active participation of many people in all sorts of irrational belief systems... Sherlock Holmes, that most famous of fictional detectives, spent a career exposing such mumbo-jumbo, but even his hard-headed empiricism is tinged with the fanciful... like Conan Doyle, Vargas presents her readers with an odd couple who have mutually antagonistic outlooks on their shared existence, and she is also concerned with the "literary" qualities of their investigations.'

Conquering Britain with Pierre Lemaitre

How easy is it to reinvigorate a shopworn formula? One way is to shoot each familiar effect full of adrenalin. The other is to inject subtly innovative elements into the detail, subverting the clichés. *Alex* by Pierre Lemaitre is a book that has it both ways, and succeeds in having its cake and eating it – yes, we've had the brutal kidnapping of a young woman before (Hans Koppel's bleak *She's Never Coming Back* and Jussi Adler-Olsen's *Mercy*, to name but two), but the victimised woman here is very different from her victimised predecessors. And although the details of her kidnapping and incarceration are familiar – as is the desperate police search to find her – Lemaitre has something very surprising up his sleeve. But is this enough to explain the feverish word-of-mouth that this book engendered?

Alex is an intriguing young woman who is introduced to us in something of a state of flux. She appears to be constantly attempting to change her identity – and her appearance – for reasons that are obscure, but seem more playful than calculated. After a flirtation with a man in a restaurant, she is assaulted and bundled into a white van where she undergoes a savage beating. The scenes of the kidnapping that follow are handled with disturbing force by the writer – however, unlike in (say) the Hans Koppel novel mentioned above, the effect of these scenes is not dispiriting, but relentlessly gripping. The man tasked with Alex's rescue is Commandant Camille Verhoerven, and we might be forgiven for thinking 'here we go again': tormented copper, personal tragedy, uneasy with subordinates. This detective, however, is something new. Verhoerven is Napoleon-sized, and congenitally stunted – and Lemaitre skilfully communicates the thought processes of a man driven by his nature to prove himself bigger than those around him in everything except height.

Familiar elements aside, it is quickly apparent that Lemaitre is worthy of all the fuss. In Frank Wynne's sympathetic translation, various subtle re-imaginings of the crime novel are handled with aplomb, such as an examination of the nature of identity (as represented by the enigmatic Alex). And Alex herself turns out to be the author's ace-in-the-hole, for reasons that will not be revealed here. By page 200 you may believe that you're moving to a pulse-raising conclusion. But you will be wrong. In some senses, the novel has only just started. Speaking to the charming, humorous Lemaitre with his UK publisher Christopher MacLehose, I found him slightly bemused by the considerable praise *Alex* had gleaned in the UK. 'I really had no idea it would be so well received in your country,' he told me. 'It's a very French book. Thank God the British really appear (against the odds) to be Francophiles!'

Pascal Garnier: Moon in a Dead Eye

The late Pascal Garnier is a leading figure in contemporary French literature. A talented novelist, short story writer, children's author and painter he published over 50 books before his untimely death in 2010. From his home in the mountains of the Ardèche, he wrote fiction using a *noir* palette with a cast of characters drawn from ordinary provincial life. Though his writing is often very dark in tone, it is infused with quirkily beautiful imagery and dry wit. Garnier's work has been likened to his great predecessor, Georges Simenon, and to the films of Tarantino and the Coen Brothers. His novels included *The Panda Theory* (2008), *How's the Pain?* (2006) and *The A26* (1999), but a good starting point for Garnier neophytes is *Moon in a Dead Eye* (2009). Given the choice, Martial would have preferred not to leave his suburban Paris life, but with all their friends moving away, or dying, his wife Odette is thrilled at the idea of moving to *Les Conviviales*, a gated retirement village in the South of France. At first, Martial's reluctance is justified. He and Odette are the only residents, and with the endless, pouring rain, he is terminally bored. With the arrival of three new neighbours and a social secretary, Martial's outlook improves and he begins to settle in to his new life. But in this isolated community, tensions are always simmering below the surface, and the arrival of some gypsies who set up camp outside the gates throws the fragile harmony into disarray. Everything comes to a head one terrible night; the night that the moon is reflected in the watchman's eye...

How's the Pain? (2006) is equally unusual. Death is Simon's business. And now the ageing vermin exterminator is preparing to die. But he still has one last job down on the coast and he needs a driver.

Bernard is twenty-one. He can drive and he's never seen the sea. He can't pass up the chance to chauffeur for Simon, whatever his mother may say. As the unlikely pair set off on their journey, Bernard soon finds that Simon's definition of vermin is broader than he'd expected... Veering from the hilarious to the horrific, this offbeat story from a master stylist is essentially an affecting study of human frailty.

Jean-Claude Izzo: Lyrical Hardboiled

Jean-Claude Izzo's *The Marseilles Trilogy* was described by *The Nation* as 'the most lyrical hardboiled writing yet', a contradictory statement with more than a grain of truth. The sequence, featuring ex-cop Fabio Montale, is a provocative and resonant classic of European crime fiction. Its publication was the catalyst for the foundation of an entire literary movement, Mediterranean Noir, and made its author an overnight celebrity. A recent reissue of the trilogy by Europa featured an introduction by a man who is arguably the reigning king of Mediterranean Noir, Massimo Carlotto. When his oldest and best friend is murdered, Fabio Montale turns his back on a police force marred by corruption and takes the fight against the local mafia into his own hands. Hard-driven protagonist aside, the real skill of the sequence lies in the evocation of Marseilles itself, its rich character fully realised.

David Platten wrote: 'The contemporary *roman noir* seems to have struck a chord with the stereotypically rebellious, middle-class teenager, who may perceive it as an iconoclastic cultural form akin to "indie" rock or underground dance music. Thus the popular French magazine *Les Inrockuptibles*, which equates to the *New Musical Express* in the UK though with a wider cultural remit, regularly carries features on the *roman noir*. However, not any *roman noir* will do. When, a few years ago, I was speaking of my interest in French crime fiction to a French university student, he fished a battered copy of a *Série noire* novel from his jacket pocket, pressed it into my hands and told me that I should forget about the writers I had just mentioned. Its title, meaningless at the time, was *Total Khéops*; the author, Jean-Claude Izzo. Although he also wrote mainstream fiction and poetry, Izzo's principal legacy is his celebrated *noir* trilogy – *Total Khéops* (1995), *Chourmo* (1996) and *Soléa* (1998) – in which he chronicles with a brutal intimacy the life of his central protagonist and first-person narrator, the disaffected crime-fighter Fabio Montale. All three novels are set in his home city of

Marseilles, which is presented in the trilogy as a topographical, historical and mythological entity. Descriptions of numerous districts flash by in a frantic present, others are coloured by events from Fabio's past or endowed with a fuller, historical definition. For Izzo, Marseilles is quintessentially a city of exiles. It stands proudly as a unique place of cultural and racial integration rather than the natural home for any one race or ethnic group... The trilogy presents an alternative mode of existence that complements the counter-culture of youth.'

Christophe Dufossé: Crime and diaphanous knickers

Is it crime fiction? Hmmm... Christophe Dufossé and his publishers practise an elaborate series of deceptions with *School's Out* (translated by Shaun Whiteside). Is this an erotic novel? The jacket seems to promise as much: a pair of female buttocks, clad in diaphanous knickers, thrusts provocatively towards us. But the book is studiedly unerotic – human feeling (physical or emotional) is ossified here, in both the teacher-narrator and his class of highly intelligent, vaguely menacing pupils. Is it a literary novel *à la* Camus? Certainly, Dufossé's countryman comes to mind while reading this haunting, allusive book, with the alienated protagonist's impressions filtered through a series of unsettling incidents, as in Camus's *The Outsider*. But the real template for *School's Out* lies in the Home Counties rather than the rural French town in which teacher and pupils clash. We encounter a class of quiet, icily polite children of fierce intelligence and terrifying force of personality – and these children sometimes speak through one member of the group, who transcribes their collective thoughts. We have a teacher, assigned to the class, who commits suicide before the narrator takes over the class from his dead colleague. Yes, it's John Wyndham's sinister sprogs from *The Midwich Cuckoos* – and in case you haven't spotted the consonance, the actor George Sanders is invoked. (Sanders played the teacher who takes his life – and the lives of his charges – in the film of Wyndham's novel, *Village of the Damned*.) Neither the come-on sexuality of the jacket nor knowledge of this award-winning debut's antecedents is much of a help in coming to grips with its obliqueness, although such an effort is definitely worthwhile. When Pierre Hoffmann inherits class 4F (boys and girls of surprising articulacy) from his colleague Eric, who has killed himself, his own life is a mess. Like his predecessor, he is someone who has not found a purpose to his existence. He resists sexual advances from both men and women, and seems to be erotically engaged only by a nurse called Nora and his own sister, now married. Pierre finds his new pupils subtly menacing, and struggles to reach them. A series of sinister incidents culminates in a coach trip with a disastrous outcome – one that leaves Pierre a different man. The themes of Dufossé's novel are many and varied: the masturbatory emptiness of modern sexuality, the uselessness of art (Pierre muses on the fact that Mahler will be known to most people through the plundering of his music for TV ads), and the nihilism of youth. But, if all this sounds rather dispiriting, the author's gift for the insightful phrase and (primarily) his teasing unfolding of a dark narrative exert a comprehensive grip. Those, however, who like their plotting pellucid need not bother.

Andrea H. Japp:
The Breath (not the Name) of the Rose

Andrea Japp's Agnès de Souarcy Chronicles are extremely individual contributions to the crowded historical crime market. (Individuality, it has to be said, is crucial in this field to rise above an army of rivals.) Set in September 1304, *The Breath of the Rose* (2009) is the perfect *entrée* to the author's vivid writing. Imprisoned by the Inquisition, Agnes de Souarcy faces interrogation and torture. At the same time, the religious community of Clairets Abbey is shaken to the core when a nun is horrifically poisoned by a murderer hidden in its midst. In this sequel to *The Season of the Beast* (2008), Andrea Japp uses her remarkable knowledge of French history and daily life in the medieval world to tell an intricate and authentic-seeming story.

Antonin Varenne: Bed of Nails

In an elegant translation by Siân Reynolds, Antonin Varenne's *Bed of Nails* (2012) proves to be something rather unusual. Varenne's work is shot through with a truly idiosyncratic vision, while also being (refreshingly) a book which is exactly as long as it needs to be – with nary a wasted word. John Nichols arrives in Paris to identify the body of an old friend, but he finds the tendrils of the late Alan Mustgrave's life extended to some surprising places. As Nichols begins to peel away the layers of mystery surrounding his dead friend, he is taken to a French capital that is most definitely off the tourist track – a place where life can be both stygian and dangerous. To some extent, Nichols is prepared for the worst – after all, his friend (it seems) bled to death during his own bizarre sadomasochistic indulgence. Also present in this murky mix is a rogue police lieutenant, Guérin, who has come to believe that the apparent suicide of Mustgrave was murder. And the unprepossessing Guérin is, in fact, one of the few honest policemen on the force. In fact, the police in this novel make the rogue cops in the TV series *Braquo* look positively squeaky-clean, and the grim legacy of police abuse (and a succession of suicides) leads to a startling conclusion, one with implications for John Nichols's own life. This is the kind of novel which has the reader eager for more work by the author, with its radical shaking-up of the detective story narrative infusing something provocative and disturbing. The French crime novel is clearly in rude health with authors such as Varenne around.

Michel Bussi: Psychological Concerns

I spoke to Kirsty Dunseath of the Orion imprint Weidenfeld & Nicolson about her foreign authors. She is the UK publisher of the Scandinavian Camilla Ceder, but is currently concentrating on French crime. She told me: 'I've just taken on a talented new French writer called Michel Bussi, whose book *Un avion sans elle*, has been a huge bestseller in France. It is a psychological thriller, more than straight crime, and wonderfully written. The novel begins with a plane crash, which one newborn baby survives, but two families (the grandfathers, in fact) step forward to claim the child. Things become dark and complicated, until a private investigator is tasked with unravelling the mystery.'

'One of the nice things about discovering new writers from Europe,' she continued, 'is that sometimes they take an established genre and give it a bit of twist, coming up with something that feels very fresh. Often that is to do with setting – helping us to see a new city or area through their eyes, or discovering the history of a place we know little about. Or it can be through character, so that we see how attitudes and preoccupations can have subtle variations within different cultures. The other side of the coin, of course, is that what may appeal to the readership within one geographical area might not translate to another; and of course you must, must, treble must have a good translator who can respond to the subtleties of a text. Thankfully there are some excellent translators out there who have the right "ear" for crime!'

In a 'pocket' guide such as this, one is always acutely conscious of omissions on the basis of space, but honourable mentions should certainly be accorded to such talented writers as **Fabrice Bourland, Philippe Claudel, Caryl Férey**, the civilised **Jean-Christophe Grangé, Eric Leclerc** (who has his own dedicated publisher in English), **Pierre Magnan, Léo Malet**, the once-popular (now neglected) espionage writer **Jean Bruce, Jean-Patrick Manchette**, the vintage writer **Hubert Monteilhet**, the economical **Daniel Pennac** and the well-regarded cult novelist **Boris Vian**.

The French Crime Screen

Despite respectable earlier entries, French crime cinema as a serious commercial entity may be said to have started with the international acclaim for the American director Jules Dassin's seminal, French-made heist movie *Rififi* in the 1950s which sired a host of progeny and opened up both a retrospective – as well as ongoing – consideration of the key crime films from France. Particular attention has long been granted to the cool, much-imitated existential tone of the Gallic crime film. Along with iconic stars associated with the genre (from the 'French Bogart', Jean Gabin, in such films as Jacques Becker's mesmeric *Touchez pas au grisbi*, to charismatic later actors such as Jean-Paul Belmondo and Alain Delon), the career of the most important director of French gangster movies, Jean-Paul Melville, is central. As is (in a different, more arthouse-oriented fashion) Claude Chabrol's upper middle-class bourgeois crime and Hitchcockery. From earlier classics such as *Pépé le Moko* and Jean Renoir's memorable 1938 version of Zola's *La bête humaine* through the *Nouvelle vague* revolution in such films as Jean-Luc Godard's *A bout de souffle/Breathless* up to pertinent modern movies such as Fred Cavayé's exciting but wearyingly unrelenting *Point Blank* (the lazily-titled French film, not the one by John Boorman with the same title), the lacerating *La haine*, *La balance* with Nathalie Baye (filmed in France by the American director Bob Swaim, which survived crass dubbing to act as a kinetic precursor to such tough TV cop shows as *Braquo*), and Jacques Audiard's inventive gangster movie *The Beat*

That My Heart Skipped (with the charismatic Roman Duris), the French crime film has ever been – and remains – pertinent, savvy and committed.

Breaking the Rules: French & Belgian Cops on TV

As well as the cinematic crime legacy, the cult appeal of gritty, often brutal French TV series must also be noted, such as the two market leaders after their showings in the UK, the uncompromising *Braquo* and *Spiral* (the latter mixing legal and police drama), with the queasy, amoral universe they inhabit making a marked contrast to the cinema equivalents and to similar shows in the UK. The levels of nihilism and corruption so endemic to these series are uniquely Gallic, and this bitter strain is also to be found in such programmes as *Gang Story* and *Paris Enquêtes Criminelles*.

Selected Films and TV (by date)

Toni (Film, 1935 Jean Renoir, director)
This landmark in French cinema presents a tawdry *crime passionel* in the naturalistic style of Marcel Pagnol. Based on a police dossier about a provincial murder, it was shot by the director's nephew, cinematographer Claude Renoir, on location (highly unusual for the time) in the small French town of Les Martigues where the actual events happened. The director's innovative use of recorded sound, authentic patois, lack of makeup and a large ensemble cast of local citizens in supporting roles have given the film the reputation of the first neo-realist movie (in fact, Visconti worked on the film). Its power may have diminished over the years, but it remains essential viewing, and it was notably under-appreciated in its day.

Pépé Le Moko (Film, 1937, Julien Duvivier, director)
An early essay in film noir, with Jean Gabin delivering a customarily low-key performance (anticipating so many actors of a later generation) as Pépé, hiding out in the unnavigable streets of the Casbah in Algiers, finding his Achilles heel in seductive tourist Mireille Balin. Duvivier's film (his best) was a blueprint for many that followed.

L'assassin habite au 21/The Murderer Lives at 21 (Film, 1942, Henri-Georges Clouzot, director)

The debut film by director Henri-Georges Clouzot, *The Murderer Lives at 21* is a brilliant hybrid of crime story and dark comedy. One of the key directors in world cinema, Henri-Georges Clouzot made a mark in 1942 with this sardonic thriller. A thief and murderer plagues the streets of Paris and is depositing a calling card from 'Monsieur Durand' at the scene of each crime. But then a cache of these cards is found by a burglar in the boarding house at 21 Avenue Junot, and Inspector Wenceslas Vorobechik (Pierre Fresnay) decides to stay at the address in a clandestine effort to solve the crimes, aided by his under-employed actress girlfriend Mila (Suzy Delair). The audacious shifts in tone from light comedy to pitch-black noir are – despite some missteps – handled with assurance by the director, as is the understated but clear picture of tensions of France under German occupation (see also *Le corbeau*, below).

Le corbeau/The Raven (Film, 1943, Henri-Georges Clouzot, director)

British cinema could claim an authentic truck drivers-in-danger film classic with Cy Endfield's *Hell Drivers*, but it would not have existed without its inspiration, Henri-Georges Clouzot's *Le salaire de la peur/ The Wages of Fear*. The latter film is much seen, and hardly neglected. Not so the rarely seen poison-pen crime drama *Le corbeau/The Raven*, another acerbic film from a director whose reputation seems to be growing stronger than ever, after its temporary eclipse in the days of the *Nouvelle vague*. During the occupation, Clouzot wrote screenplays and directed for the German-owned company Continental Films. His second film, *Le corbeau*, was excoriated for its unsparing vision of provincial France, and Continental fired the director. The film has been subsequently reappraised as an examination of collective guilt and complaisance with evil; but, despite the intervention of his Jewish friends, Clouzot was barred from making films until 1947 by the French government. Otto Preminger re-made the film in Hollywood, but, ruthlessly unsentimental director though he was, Hollywood censorship of the day would not allow the frankness of Clouzot's blistering original – the eroticism and abortion themes were unacceptable. *Le corbeau*, a dark and subversive study of human nature, stars Pierre Fresnay and Ginette Leclerc. A wave of hysteria sweeps the small provincial town of St Robin when a series of poison-pen letters signed 'Le corbeau' (The Raven) denounces several prominent members of society. Starting with the village doctor, the sinister trickle of letters soon becomes a flood, and no one is safe from the malicious accusations, which include abortion and drug addiction. The film was condemned by the political left and right and the church upon its release in 1943.

Thérèse Raquin (Film, 1953, Marcel Carné, director)

Emile Zola's powerful novel of death and adultery *Thérèse Raquin* is given a (then) modern day makeover in this 1953 adaptation which is much admired – not surprisingly, given that Carné has the memorable Simone Signoret and Raf Vallone as the tormented lovers paying a price for their passion. But there is strong work, too, from Jacques Duby as the sickly, doomed husband. This is among the director's best work from the 1950s, along with such films as *L'air de Paris*.

Touchez pas au grisbi/Hands off the Loot (Film, 1954, Jacques Becker, director)

Jean Gabin's performance as the past-his-best, ageing criminal Max in Jacques Becker's *Touchez pas au grisbi* (aka *Hands off the Loot* – a title which hardly possesses the ring of the original) is absolutely emblematic, and sums up all the world-weary, rugged appeal that the actor projected throughout his lengthy career. After executing the heist of a lifetime, Max is looking forward to enjoying the spoils with his seductive young girlfriend. But when his undisciplined partner and friend Riton (René Dary) allows news of the robbery to leak to the untrustworthy Josy (the matchless Jeanne Moreau), Max finds himself drawn back into a world he has tried to leave. In terms of its cynical (if non-judgemental) acceptance of a world of compromise and professional criminality, it's hard to imagine a film which so successfully channels this dark and bitter world.

Les diaboliques/The Fiends (Film, 1954, Henri-Georges Clouzot, director)

As well as being one of the most effective films in crime cinema – a piece that still carries a charge even in our seen-it-all era – Clouzot's classic was ground-breakingly influential. Its grim bathroom shenanigans, for instance, remain flesh-creeping, despite endless borrowings. Apart from the matchless black-and-white cinematography, it is, of course, the impeccable performances that still register: a glowering Simone Signoret, a sneering Paul Meurisse, and (most memorably) Vera Clouzot's vulnerability as the terrified wife. Nepotism (for once) earns an honourable place here with Clouzot's casting of his wife. A forgettable American re-make with Sharon Stone can be... forgotten.

Rififi/Du Rififi chez les hommes (Film, 1955, Jules Dassin, director)

It doesn't date an iota – and, in fact, Jules Dassin's richly textured *Du Rififi chez les hommes* makes Guy Ritchie and other perpetrators of screen heists and criminals falling out with each other look like small beer indeed. Acknowledged as the forerunner of, and inspiration behind, many modern day crime capers (including, most notably, *The Usual Suspects* and *Reservoir Dogs*), Dassin's French noir classic remains the quintessential heist movie, not least for Jean Servais' bitter, ageing thief and its celebrated, much-imitated wordless robbery sequence (the one with the umbrella passed through a hole drilled in the ceiling to catch falling plaster). A word of caution which is perhaps unnecessary for readers of this book: be sure to seek out the version with the original French dialogue. Anyone who's suffered the crassly dubbed horror that has circulated in the past will appreciate that advice.

Classe tous risques/Consider All Risks (Film, 1960, Claude Sautet, director)

A film much praised by an impressive trio of authoritative filmmakers – Jean-Pierre Melville, Robert Bresson and Bertrand Tavernier. The latter noted, 'We've come to understand that *Classe tous risques* ... was just as revolutionary as *Breathless* ... Sautet was renewing the genre, profoundly, from the inside, instantly turning dozens of contemporary films into dusty relics.' One of the most surprising things about Sautet's sinewy film, excavated by the BFI in 2013, is the neglect of a classic French crime movie. The directorial debut of Claude Sautet (1924 – 2000), better known for his later films *Un coeur en hiver* (1992) and *Nelly et Monsieur Arnaud* (1995), *Classe tous risques* stars the great Italian-born character actor Lino Ventura as Abel Davos, a once powerful Parisian gangster, convicted of multiple crimes in France and sentenced to death *in absentia*, who has grown weary of his Italian exile and longs to return home with his wife and two small children. In order to finance this ambition, he decides to pull one last job – boldly executed in broad daylight on the streets of Milan – before heading in the direction of Nice.

The getaway proves highly perilous, and Abel realises that he will never make it to Paris without a little help from his friends. But his old pals and partners-in-crime – despite the formidable debt they all owe him – are reluctant to risk their own safety. Instead they send a complete stranger, the fresh-faced Eric Stark (the young, then-unknown Jean-Paul Belmondo), to escort their former comrade from Nice to Paris. Scored in uncharacteristic fashion by Georges Delerue and shot in expressive black and white by Ghislain Cloquet (later to win an Oscar for Polanski's *Tess*), *Classe tous risques* is based on a novel by death-row-inmate-turned-writer José Giovanni (*Le trou*, *Le deuxième souffle*) whose intimate knowledge of the underworld lends an authenticity. Suspenseful and frequently moving, the film is a study of loyalty and betrayal, distinguished by a bleak, incisive psychological truth. The relative obscurity of Sautet's thriller is in many ways an accident of history. It was simply swept away in the frenzy of excitement generated by the *Nouvelle vague* which made its classical virtues appear old-fashioned. Released in Paris in March 1960, it was almost immediately overshadowed by Godard's *Breathless* (Belmondo's international breakthrough) which opened a week later.

Pleins feux sur l'assassin/Spotlight on a Murderer (Film, 1960, Georges Franju, director)

Franju's gruesome (and poetically beautiful) masterpiece *Les yeux sans visage* has long enjoyed a high reputation, but a great deal of his remarkable output remains unseeable in the early twenty-first century. Franju aficionados can only yearn for the day when such films as *Pleins feux sur l'assassin* become once again available. (This neglect is not just in America and the UK: even in France, Franju's countrymen have not made his work available.) Pierre Boileau, no less, is responsible for the screenplay for *Pleins feux sur l'assassin*, clearly designed to be sufficiently dyspeptic to appeal to the cynical Franju. The blackly comic narrative has Count Hervé de Kéraudren opting to hide himself in a secret alcove when his time comes because he is determined to die in a way calculated to confound his heirs. Because his corpse is not discovered, the relatives are obliged to cool their heels for five years until they can inherit their dead relative's legacy – though they are obliged to maintain the Kéraudren estate. To fund the latter, the relatives put together a Son et Lumière display while still searching for the missing body. But then they begin to die, one by one...

Que la bête meure/Killer (Film, 1969, Claude Chabrol, director)

Despite being the most ambitious director of the French *Nouvelle vague* in terms of diversity of subject, Claude Chabrol fell from favour with his *Cahiers du Cinéma* colleagues who felt that his fondness for sampling popular genres had cost him his *auteur* credentials. Chabrol had, in fact, made what is customarily regarded as the film that inaugurated the movement, *Le beau Serge* (1958). Subsequently, he was forgiven his straying from the fold (and his long-term tendency to encourage the broadest, virtually parodic playing in his secondary characters) for the films of his lengthy Indian Summer. Chabrol came to be seen as the definitive cinematic anatomiser of the crises of the middle classes, through a prism of wry affection mixed with contempt. The director, one of the many Gallic disciples of Alfred Hitchcock, had always nourished a taste for the crime and thriller genre, and one of his most intriguing essays in this area was a cool and compelling take on Nicholas Blake's *The Beast Must Die* (*Que la bête meure*), noted for its remarkable use of Brahms's Four Serious Songs, sung by Kathleen Ferrier. Chabrol has the full measure of this classic British crime novel and translates its nihilistic tone effortlessly to a Mediterranean setting. While other directors of the French New Wave fell by the wayside, Chabrol consolidated his career longevity by making this kind of crime cinema his special preserve.

Le cercle rouge (Film, 1970, Jean-Pierre Melville, director)

There was a time when Jean-Pierre Melville's remarkable and influential Gallic noir was all-but-unseeable apart from the celebrated *Le Samourai*. Thankfully, a slew of DVD issues is remedying that lamentable situation with splendid new transfers. *Le cercle rouge* is one of Melville's most imposing essays in the genre, featuring two icons of French cinema: Alain Delon and Yves Montand. Both are encouraged by the director to give frigid, affectless performances which are totally apposite in this tale of casual death and criminality. Delon's character, fresh out of jail, double-crosses a mob boss and commits a jewel robbery. Despite the suppressed desperation of the protagonists, the films of Melville – cool and ambiguous – represent the French gangster film at its most pared-down and allusive.

Diva (Film, 1981, Jean-Jacques Beineix, director)

The stylish, glossy (and superficial) crime novels by the pseudonymous 'Delacorta' may have had a short shelf life, but they did manage to engender this cult film which matched its seductive source, all glittering surfaces, memorable soundtrack and cool attitudes. A young opera-obsessive bootlegs the work of an American soprano, but the tape gets juggled with another implicating a police chief in mob involvement. An aria from Alfredo Catalani's neglected opera La Wally is used repeatedly (and to mesmerising effect), achieving a new fame.

Dobermann (Film, 1997, Jan Kounen, director)

Fasten your seat belts. Husband and wife team, tough Vincent Cassel and voluptuous Monica Bellucci, ensure that Jan Kounen's stylish, violent, distinctly non-reflective action movie about bank robbers on the run is always exhilarating – if finally, with its unrelenting accelerando tempo and almost complete lack of nuance and shading, somewhat exhausting. The animated credit sequence is a key to the outrageous tone.

Baise-moi (Film, 2000, Virginie Despentes & Coralie Trinh Thi, directors)

Let's be honest: right from the start, along with its variety of other objectives, it has always been the job of cinema to shock. And there is no question that this controversial, deeply nihilistic film – which has not a single sympathetic character, male or female – does just that. If you prefer your cinema graphic and unstinting, then this is very much a piece for you. Absolutely nothing in terms of violence and unsimulated sex is spared. But, if you favour cosier viewing, perhaps you should steer well clear. Baise-moi may now be seen completely uncut. The film has been characterised (accurately) as Thelma and Louise on acid with its two grubby and murderous anti-heroines bloodily cutting down (or having rough sex with) pretty well anyone they encounter. It was banned upon its initial release in its native France in 2000 for its refusal to look away from any action – the couplings, though explicit, are notably (and deliberately) joyless.

Engrenages/Spiral (TV, 2005–, Philippe Triboit, Pascal Chaumiel et al, directors)

After the unprecedented success of the Danish crime series The Killing, there was a scramble to find something similar for UK audiences – a foreign detective series which treats its audience with intelligence, and offers genuine texture and complexity. In fact, that show was already around, and *Spiral* has subsequently enjoyed a similar word-of-mouth success (if without quite the cult following the Danish show gleaned). So the DVD issues have been a welcome chance to rediscover just what was quite so special about this French series. *Spiral* has been gradually building up a reputation over several well-received seasons. At the centre of this gritty, authentic show is police captain Laure Bethaud. She is very ably played by Caroline Proust, who makes Laure conflicted, driven, tough and vulnerable; it is a performance of considerable range and achievement. Laure is uninterested in the conventional feminine virtues, driving herself and her team with unsparing energy. And as the increasingly hard-edged episodes show, this is a series both written and cast from strength. Caroline Proust is surrounded by a flintily-characterised dramatis personae, notably Audrey Fleurot as the corrupt, flame-haired advocate Joséphine Karlsson. The series has a powerful plot strand set in the world of French jurisprudence and Karlsson finds – painfully – that lying down with dogs is a sure way of acquiring fleas. If you're feeling deprived of the kind of fix that you used to get from Sarah Lund, then *Spiral* – and the no-nonsense but desperate Laure Bethaud – will be right up your alley.

Caché/Hidden (Film, 2005, Michael Haneke, director)
If you haven't already been seduced by the remarkable word-of-mouth success of Michael Haneke's characteristically disturbing thriller, you can have little interest in contemporary cinema. The director's challenging earlier films have ratcheted up the possibilities of the psychological drama to new heights of intensity, heavy with violent emotion, and the success this film enjoyed was well deserved. Daniel Auteil plays a television presenter who begins to receive mysterious and alarming packages containing covertly filmed videos of himself and his family. Sinister phone calls follow, and it is impossible not to identify with the family under siege, as Haneke combines Hitchcockian tension with cool arthouse refinement.

The Beat That My Heart Skipped (Film, 2005, Jacques Audiard, director)
This remake of James Toback's 1978 film *Fingers* manages (against the odds) to match its source, with Romain Duris replacing Harvey Keitel as a collector for the mob keen to leave behind his violent life and become a concert pianist. It's a dark study of malign fate and aspiration set against the appeal of great music.

Ne le dis à personne/Tell No One (Film, 2006, Guillaume Canet, director)

It can happen: a film can actually do full justice to a book – in this case, a French film of an American novel. With every succeeding book, US writer Harlan Coben has conjured up clever challenges for his sports agent/detective, Myron Bolitar. In crackling prose, Coben has taken Myron on some wild rides, but most admirers of the writer believe his best work to be in standalones such as *Tell No One*. Guillaume Canet's adroitly directed film has the measure of the material here. The book's protagonists, David and Elizabeth Beck. become Alexandre and Margot. She is murdered, and Alexandre is left for dead, although he is the prime suspect for the murder. For the next eight years, he attempts to come to terms with the horror of this catastrophe, but then his world is destabilised by a bizarre series of events. Is Elizabeth – somehow – alive? Beck finds the few remaining shreds of his life torn apart as he tries to track down a ghost whose message to him has been a warning: tell no one. Canet's film is a lean and mercurial narrative, delivered with panache by a genuine stylist of the thriller genre, and Coben aficionados were grateful that the writer had enjoyed a very solid adaptation, perhaps even helped by the shift in locale.

Mesrine 1 & 2 (Film, 2008, Jean-François Richet, director)

This uncompromising two-part French gangster film arrived in the UK festooned with praise, and had already evoked comparisons with the crime epics of Coppola and Scorsese. The two films which combine to tell this lacerating story are both acerbic examples of the genre, but also a provocative examination of the nature of celebrity – something that the violent and charismatic Mesrine himself cultivated. The two films were based on the gangster Mesrine's memoirs. The first film shows his violent ascent to the upper echelons of the criminal world, while its successor describes his life after he has been declared Public Enemy No.1 in France, concluding with his inevitable fall. In a media-savvy age, director Jean-François Richet focuses on the character's manipulation of the media (finessing his synthetic image of a rebel against the system), and turns this plot point to advantage to forge a commentary on celebrity and its manipulability. Inevitably films such as *Mesrine* depend for their success upon the impact of their principal performers, and Vincent Cassel perfectly incarnates both the charisma and the reptile ruthlessness of the subject although, even over two lengthy films, the gangster (it has to be said) remains relatively one-dimensional.

State Affairs (Film, 2009, Éric Valette, director)

Éric Valette was also responsible for directing some of the episodes of the tough and uncompromising French TV cop series *Braquo*. Adapted from award-winning French writer Dominique Manotti's novel about killings linking an arms-dealing middleman to French political power, *State Affairs* features some of the most promising young French actors, along with the reliably world-weary André Dussollier. It is a suspenseful and finely-honed piece built around three principal characters: a corrupt politician, his utterly ruthless hitman employee and an equally hard-boiled (if novice) female cop. Two violent events set the narrative in motion: a plane exploding above the Gulf of Guinea, and the brutal murder of a prostitute. Despite the thousands of miles separating these two events, single-minded Parisian policewoman Nora Chahyd ignores a lack of cooperation from her superiors in order to make the connections (which, of course, are hidden but present). Soon, Nora finds herself in the middle of a labyrinthine government cover-up which extends to the very top of French society. Compelling though this is, the film is to some extent a victim of its own crowded scenario and the director's obvious pleasure in the surprising narrative twists. Éric Valette was able to better balance such felicities against a forensic concentration on character (given the extra running time) in *Braquo*, making the latter still his most impressive work. This remains worthwhile stuff.

Braquo (TV, 2009, Olivier Marchal, director)

If you consider yourself an aficionado of the most uncompromising crime series on TV and you haven't yet watched *Braquo*, then you're missing something. This flint-edged, dyspeptic and utterly compelling series (often described as the French equivalent of *The Wire*) is so uncompromising – even nihilistic – in its view of French police work that it makes such gritty rivals as *Spiral* look positively rose-coloured. Apart from its impeccable ensemble playing (with Jean-Hugues Anglade as mesmerising as ever – and stoking down his customary easy charm – in the role of a compromised Parisian cop finding himself drawn ever deeper into realms of corruption and violence after the suicide of the leader of his squad), the really provocative aspect of the series lies not so much in the visceral impact of the filmmaking but in the uneasy dialectic it orchestrates with the viewer. It's a measure of the sheer skill of *Braquo* that most viewers will spend their time veering between being on the side of the French cops as they perform another outrageous, ill-advised stunt (including armed robbery) or shouting at the screen: 'What are you doing?' Never comfortable viewing, the series is essential for those who favour the equation: crime drama=strong meat.

Black Heaven (Film, 2010, Gilles Marchand, director)
This visually seductive French thriller, in which a naïve young man is ensnared by a seductive woman, is as unorthodox in its approach as one might expect from the director of the outrageous *Who Killed Bambi*? Such is the indebtedness of the team which created this to the surrealistic grotesqueries of David Lynch that echoes of that director's *Blue Velvet* are not hard to discern in this highly unusual piece.

The Assault (Film, 2010, Julien Leclercq, director)
Perhaps the most striking thing about this gripping and unrelenting hostage drama is its refusal to bow to any notions of political correctness in an era of caution. The fundamentalist inspiration of the terrorists who take over a plane is given little shrift (or sympathy) here, with a willingness to die in the name of any deity a particular target for the director and writer's disdain. Perhaps the SWAT team sent against the terrorists might have been characterised with more imagination, but there is no denying the fact that the tension is rigorously maintained.

Salamander (TV, 2012, Frank van Mechelen, director)
Such is the English taste for European crime drama that there was a ready audience for this Belgian thriller shown in 2014. The solidly-made, slightly stolid series utilises the familiar ingredients of a bloody-minded copper at odds with his superiors. In a private Brussels bank, 66 safe-deposit boxes are raided. The owner of the bank wants to keep the thefts under wraps but police inspector Paul Gerardi (Filip Peeters) catches wind of the affair. With his incorruptible, old-school morals, Gerardi throws himself into the investigation, and when some of the key players are murdered, commit suicide or vanish, soon realises just how big the case is. Gerardi discovers that the victims are members of a secret organisation called Salamander, made up of the country's industrial, financial, judicial and political elite. Strong stuff. But there are caveats, however; it's not quite clear how we are supposed to regard this supposedly intelligent protagonist who again and again uncaringly puts his family in danger by his ignore-all-warnings attitude – and there is a paucity of strongly written female characters. But despite its conventional structure, the show possesses qualities which command the attention throughout.

GERMANY, AUSTRIA AND SWITZERLAND

Murder in the German–speaking territories

The immense popularity of crime fiction in those countries which speak German (Germany itself, Switzerland and Austria) is a phenomenon noted throughout Europe, with several writers from other countries (notably the Scandinavian territories) enjoying far greater sales in that country than, for instance, in Britain. Many German names have been given to the genre, but the one which has had the most traction is simply 'Krimi.' Earliest examples of the genre in the eighteenth and nineteenth centuries often utilised the 'police report' format which had also been popular in Britain. Subsequently, a variety of German writers in the early twentieth century began to create something like an indigenous genre including individual talents such as Karl Rosner and Baldwin Groller (the latter, in fact, an Austrian writer).

Shadow of the Four Just Men

The inexplicably long shadow in German of the British crime writer Edgar Wallace (in translation) must be noted. His work has had a popularity long outlasting his readership in the UK where his crudely written crime novels are largely unread today. This has been complemented by a long-running series of film adaptations of his work by various studios, dispatched in appropriately unsubtle fashion. Many of these films present a singularly quaint, utterly unreal vision of London.

At the middle of the last century, one of the most enduring contributions to the genre was created by the Swiss writer **Friedrich Dürrenmatt**, with his excellent *The Judge and his Hangman* (1963) and *The Pledge* (1959), both of which infused the crime story with a genuine philosophical import in the manner of his plays. So too, in different fashion, did the writers **Peter Handke** and **Heinrich Böll**, adding provocative layers of social criticism.

Norbert Jacques' series concerning the criminal mastermind Dr Mabuse (one of the prototypes for Ian Fleming's megalomaniac villains) is perhaps better known through the films directed by Fritz Lang and other less talented filmmakers but, by the beginning of the twenty-first century, the 'Krimi' genre was enjoying even greater popularity with several hundred writers listed in a variety of bibliographic sources. A stellar name in this company is **Pieke Biermann**, responsible for a series of adroitly-written Berlin-set police procedurals featuring Chief Inspector Karen Litze. And there's the popular work of **Charlotte Link**, as well as **Patrick Süskind's** cult historical novel *Perfume*. It has become more and more apparent in recent writing that the legacy of Germany's wartime past is moving centre stage as a subject for many writers (a syndrome also noted in the work of several Nordic crime novelists), as is a noirish satirical infusion provided by such writers as **Simon Urban** in *Plan D* (2013) and other books. Of Urban, Harvill Secker's senior crime editor Alison Hennessey has provided an encomium, but first I asked her about publishing crime in translation in general. 'For me,' she said, 'the joys of publishing European authors in translation are the same as with publishing all authors: introducing readers to a wonderful new writer. Depending on the particular book or author, you may also be shedding light on a world or society that is relatively less well known in the UK – or using a wonderfully gripping plot to explore wider issues. I really enjoyed publishing Simon Urban's German language thriller *Plan D*, for example, because it had a very clever premise – what would Germany be like if the Berlin Wall had never fallen? – but it also explored ideas of democracy and dictatorships in a way that was interesting and accessible to all.'

Speaking to the knowledgeable writer and translator Almuth Heuner about the German crime scene – and the plans for this book – was, as I expected, highly instructive.

'I notice,' she told me, 'that you plan to mention Handke, Böll, Fallada and Jelinek. Fine, but I'd note that they are usually not considered as crime writers in Germany, but as "literary writers". You wouldn't find them in crime and mystery sections in bookshops.'

'One novelist I'd like to extol the virtues of is **Akif Pirincci** who has been translated into English with at least one book, *Felidae*. That novel may not initially inspire, looking like a simple cat mystery, but it really is a very dark noir in the classic tradition of Hammett. And there's **Ingrid Noll**, who is something of a grand old lady, but it should be noted that she started publishing novels at a later age than most. She's very well known in Germany, and has been translated into English. Her writing is a little like Barbara Vine (but she's a much more concise novelist). **Petra Hammesfahr**, also translated, writes a little like Nele Neuhaus (who I believe you interviewed onstage at Harrogate concerning her novel *Snow White Must Die*), and has been around much longer than Nele. Petra is very popular. And as you're including Austria with Germany, **Wolf Haas** is a much-respected Austrian crime novelist, though it has to be admitted that his work is not to everyone's taste.'

Almuth concurred with calling this section 'Germany/Austria/ Switzerland'. 'Friedrich Dürrenmatt, another more literary writer,' she said, 'is less a crime writer than someone in the literary/dramatic tradition – and, of course, he is Swiss. Of course, the most prominent German-writing Swiss was **Friedrich Glauser** whom we consider as something like our crime/mystery patron saint (and we have named our prestigious Glauser awards in his honour). His novels are translated into English, and his reputation is assured.

'As the book market in Germany is really the only German-speaking one that counts in all important aspects, it's not really possible to divide the German-speaking – and writing – scene into the various countries. Roughly, Austria contributes about 5 per cent and German-speaking Switzerland about 3 per cent of all authors, books, publishers, readers. And the contribution – in monetary terms – is actually less than that percentage. Luxembourg, Liechtenstein and German-speaking Belgium are so small in terms of contributions that they are nearly non-existent in all of the categories mentioned above. And – note that I don't say this because I'm chauvinistic – I conducted a very thorough survey two years ago, expecting to discover different figures, but the ones I found were actually even lower than I suspected.

'It's infuriating that so few of our really accomplished authors can be read in English translation. Under these limiting circumstances, our crime scene must look rather minor and unimpressive to the English-speaking reader, and those that are translated don't show the variety of styles and topics and sub-genres we can lay claim to. But obviously – in the real world – there's nothing to be done about this. The English-speaking market is so saturated, and one has to admit that Germany doesn't look quite as sexy as Sweden or Italy. And, let's be frank, those countries have a huge market in Germany. Germans do buy and read these foreign books. There's no arguing with that, however proud we may be of our own writers.'

Nele Neuhaus: Snow White Must Die

It may be a cliché to say that Nele Neuhaus stormed the bestseller charts with her crime series featuring investigative team DI Pia Kirchhoff and DS Oliver von Bodenstein, but that is exactly what she did. From the vagaries of self-publishing, she has moved on to the real thing, selling over 3 million copies in Germany alone, and she is now published in 21 countries. The first book in her sequence, *Snow White Must Die* (2013, Macmillan), is a tour-de-force that begins in a small German town in which a boy is accused of murdering his seductive girlfriend, the 'Snow White' of the title, and very dark deeds are done against the setting of beautiful German countryside. This first book has British readers keenly anticipating its successor.

The young man, Tobias, convicted for murder, does his time, but on his return to his village is something of a pariah, and his presence begins to stir up secrets from the past. But it's clear that there are many who would prefer those secrets to stay buried. Tobias and his family are subjected to vicious attacks, and after the disinterring of a young girl's skeleton, DI Pia Kirchhoff and DS Oliver von Bodenstein are given the task of monitoring the incendiary atmosphere in the town. It becomes clear that the mystery of the disappearance of 'Snow White' has tendrils that reach into the present.

Neuhaus instantly establishes her authority by taking things very much at their own pace, and the steady accretion of detail is done with quiet skill. In a translation by Steven T Murray (who, of course, rendered the vengeful activities of Lisbeth Salander into English), a powerful grip is exerted even in the teeth of a great variety of German names and characters which require close attention by the reader. The close-mouthed village clearly practises a Sicilian code of Omertà, and the relentless unpeeling of layers of deception is set against the adroit characterisation of the police and their relationships (Oliver's marriage is under strain because of his wife's eccentric behaviour). It's not hard to see why Neuhaus is achieving pole position among European crime writers. While the specifically German character of the novel is undeniable, it is universal in its application, and there are occasional reminiscences of writers of other countries – Stieg Larsson, for instance, and even Ian Rankin.

Speaking to Nele Neuhaus, I discovered that the writer herself possesses an internationalist approach; although she feels at home in such quintessentially German cities as Hamburg ('Still exciting for me!'), the influences that have shaped her are largely speaking from other countries. If the writer's own sardonic humour – evident in any conversation with her – is perhaps less in evidence in her writing, that is because she has an ambitious approach to the crime novel. However, the seriousness of her work is never ponderous despite the Teutonic stereotypes that exist in the minds of many non-Germans. 'I'm interested in character, first and foremost', she told me. 'Everything else has to be at the service of that.'

Jan Costin Wagner: Breaking the Silence

Is Jan Costin Wagner part of the Scandinavian new wave? Or a German writer who just happens to move (profitably) in this territory? In fact, the novelist, born in Langen near Frankfurt in 1972, metaphorically resides in the best of both worlds. His series featuring Finnish detective Kimmo Joentaa quickly established itself as one of the most distinctive in the field, with such intricate books as *Ice Moon* (2006, Vintage, translated by John Brownjohn) and the ambitious and complex *Silence* (2011, Vintage, translated by Anthea Bell), which was made into a film directed by Baran bo Odar and shown on BBC4 in 2013 (see below). Wagner's grasp of the darker aspects of human psychology is unsparing, and renders his books as unsettling as they are hypnotic. While he is perfectly happy to be identified as part of the Nordic Noir wave, the writer makes no claim to a Scandinavian identity. He told me that he felt a writer should rise above limiting national characteristics and confront the real business of human nature, business that transcends national characteristics and that each author is obliged to deal with in their own way. He is similarly less interested in the locales of his books (although they are evocatively created) and feels that his real subject is the interior lives of his characters, whatever the land of their birth. Finland, however, is his chosen literary stomping ground and in such books as *The Winter of the Lions* (2011, Harvill Secker, translated by Anthea Bell), he is interested in the constraints of the media-savvy world we all live in today, one in which the specious morality propounded by politicians, newspaper and television pundits rules the roost. The thorny problem of a rush to judgement in so many areas is a theme he deals with rigorously in several of his novels, notably in *Silence* with its paedophilia motifs.

'I'm intrigued by the way in which justice can be done,' he told me, 'even when the timescale involved is longer than we might like it to be. *Silence*, for instance, has two horrendous crimes separated by two decades, but there is a resolution of sorts. In this I am perhaps influenced by a favourite writer of mine, Friedrich Dürrenmatt, whose *The Pledge* deals rigorously with the consequences of a crime stretching over many years – and its delayed final resolution. I'm also fascinated by the very bleak worldview found in the novels of Patricia Highsmith.' Wagner does not try to force the narrative development. 'I try to allow the books to take precisely the time that is required to tell the tales', he said, 'the approach, in fact, of my detective Kimmo Joentaa.' He sidesteps the conventional imperatives of the crime novel to confront the reader with a more complex experience. 'Literature,' he said, 'can anatomise society. And crime fiction is able to channel the basic fears and hopes of our fraught contemporary life. I don't trust newspapers,' he continues, 'and I believe that an intuitive analysis of the modern world is possible through fiction.' His multi-country connections have allowed him to present a truly pan-European vision of society.

The writer clearly respects his readers' intelligence particularly in the area of not providing easy (and lazy) frissons, preferring to work on the creation of an all-pervasive layer of dread. *Light in a Dark House* (Harvill Secker, 2013, translated by Anthea Bell) is the fourth of his Kimmo Joentaa novels, and begins with an unidentified woman in a coma being murdered, the sheets on her bed stained by her murderer's tears. This is uncompromising, astringent crime writing of a rare order.

Criminal Therapy with Sebastian Fitzek

When Sebastian Fitzek's novel *Therapy* (2008, translated by Sally-Ann Spencer) dislodged *The Da Vinci Code* from the number one book chart position in Germany, attention began to be paid to a writer who was clearly doing something unusual, shaking up the psychological crime genre and producing something rich and strange. Subsequent books by Fitzek, including *The Eye Collector* (2013, Corvus, translated by John Brownjohn), have maintained his upward trajectory. *Splinter* (2011) is a key Fitzek novel. Suffering agonies of guilt after an accident has brought about the death of his wife and unborn child, Marc Lucas is living in a kind of daze. He returns home one night to discover that his key no longer fits in the lock. More shockingly, his wife is alive and pregnant but says that she does not recognise him. This is the beginning of a nightmare experience for Lucas, where reality and dream merge in the most disturbing of fashions. What will be the cost – his sanity? Sebastian Fitzek here demonstrates more than a touch of the ingenious narrative skill of Harlan Coben.

Sebastian Fitzek was born in Berlin in 1971 and worked as a journalist before writing *Therapy*. This debut was shortlisted for the Friedrich Glauser Prize (the principal award for best German crime novel) and pleased both critics and readers alike. Eight subsequent bestsellers cemented his reputation as a star of German thriller-writing – and 2013's *The Sleepwalker* was a *Spiegel* no.1 bestseller. Fitzek's books have been translated into over twenty languages, have been adapted for the stage, and one of them, *The Child*, has been made into a film. Significantly, Fitzek is one of the (relatively) few recent German thriller writers to have been published in Britain.

The writer is particularly interested in the ways in which the trauma of crime leaves scars on the human soul, and *The Eye Collector* has a past-his-best policeman (turned journalist) on the trail of a truly nasty serial killer. It's a ticking clock scenario that really does have the reader's palms sweating. Fitzek's work as a journalist (he is currently head of programming at Berlin's leading radio station) has given him an unerring grasp of the way human beings behave *in extremis*, even those of us who would not describe ourselves as criminally inclined. Talking to him about his work, I found a disarming mix of frankness and insight. I asked if crime fiction can make serious points about modern German society.

'Definitely!' he replied firmly. 'Not only *can* it do so, but I think that serious crime writing *should* do so. In fact, I've noticed that some authors pick provocative themes which are relevant to the society long before they are treated in any other entertainment media.

'Take, for example, child abuse. In Germany, you can watch dozens of crime movies every day on television, many of them produced in Germany, such as those in the most popular format, *Tatort*, with over 10 million viewers. But the stories hardly ever engage with such difficult issues as paedophilia or modern slavery. This is a significant problem in Germany, principally due to the fact that prostitution is not illegal. It's this fact that makes it very easy for the organised crime rings to make massive profits in this area. But, frankly, television tends to steer clear of such topics. They are often a no-go area because the editors and producers have persuaded themselves that female viewers don't want to hear about those "hard topics". But I've tried to make sure that my own crime literature deals very specifically with those themes and makes them central. It's a writer's duty to allow readers a view behind the curtain, particularly when some people don't welcome such frankness. Even – dare I say it – some over-cautious publishers?'

Surely, I suggest (playing devil's advocate), publishers know what their readers want?

'When I pitched the story of my third book, *The Child*, in 2007,' he replies, 'my publisher was not sure if female readers would want to read about child molestation. But that is to seriously underestimate women readers. Of course they're prepared to accept such subjects, if they realise that the writer is not interested in simply shocking the reader but is interested in providing insights into such crimes – and the way society deals with such incendiary issues. Good crime literature is fake, of course. We – the authors – make it all up. But as with every good lie, there has to be a truthful core at the centre. This core is often an unblinking description of modern society with all its perplexing problems.'

Talking about *Splinter*, Fitzek observed: 'Usually, thrillers dealing with loss of memory are about a character trying to retrieve his memories. In *Splinter*, I took a different path by asking: what if we could erase the worst memories of our lives – forever? What would happen if we had the opportunity to induce selective amnesia? And what would happen, if – as I describe in *Splinter* – something went wrong during this psychiatric experiment? The idea for the book came to me after I'd had a conversation with an eccentric neurosurgeon who said to me: "Most people are looking for methods to memorise things ever faster. But a few are looking for a method to *forget*." Personally, I'd be really nervous of undertaking a psychiatric experiment such as this. I'd be afraid what would happen to me would be exactly what happens to the hero of my psychothriller: that I would lose the ability to distinguish between illusion and reality and my life would – yes, splinter completely. Memories configure our identity, and we would erase them at our peril. Although, there are (of course) some experiences in my life which I would dearly like to forget...'

Hans Fallada: Alone In Berlin

There are crime elements to be found in one of the most significant and highly-regarded of German novels. Berlin in 1940 is a city living in threat and terror. The various people at 55 Jablonski Strasse have different strategies for coping with the increasingly brutal Nazi rule. Frau Rosenthal suffers, her nervous disposition not suited to the times; the Persickes revel in their enthusiastic support for Hitler, browbeating those around them; the Quangels are struggling to come to terms with the death of their son; and the quietly spoken Otto decides to act against the barbarism. Primo Levi called *Alone in Berlin* the greatest book ever written about German resistance to the Nazis, and it is still an excoriating (if demanding) novel of weight and intelligence.

Elfriede Jelinek: Greed

The work of the Nobel Prize-winning Austrian playwright and novelist Elfriede Jelinek is marked by her political stance. Her espousal of feminism and her individual interpretation of the tenets of the Communist Party are keys to her work, and her stated target – the capitalist consumer society – aligns her work with that of the Swedes Maj Sjöwall and Per Wahlöö, who shared many of her views. The preoccupations of another Swedish writer, Stieg Larsson, are echoed in Jelinek's concern for the exploitation of women in what she (and Larsson) saw as a misogynist, phallocratic society. In *Greed* (2006), the protagonist is country policeman Kurt Janisch, frustrated at the lack of progress in his career. He finds himself talking to a great many women, some of them middle-aged and unfulfilled like himself, and several fall under his spell. When a murder takes place (with a body in a lake) Kurt's already tangled life becomes even more complicated. In many ways, this is a psychological crime novel of the kind the publisher Serpent's Tail has made very much their own, and any reader pointed to the book by the publisher's name will not be disappointed. But as well as an unsparing analysis of the characters, there is that remarkable sense of place in which the author excels – the mountains and towns of southern Austria have rarely been so effectively conjured. And the author's customary sociopolitical concerns are just underneath the surface.

The Jakob Arjouni Phenomenon

There are few crime fiction aficionados – at least those in the know – who would deny that one of the most significant of German crime writers was a coruscating talent who died far too young. Achieving literary success at the precipitate age of 20 is not always the soundest of moves, but Jakob Arjouni parlayed it into a highly successful career, leaving behind an impressive corpus of novels at his death at the age of 48. (The similarly short-lived Stieg Larsson at least reached his half century.) These books included five quirky private eye novels which featured his Turkish detective working in Frankfurt, Kemal Kayankaya. The most notable of these was *Happy Birthday, Turk!*, written in 1987 and filmed in 1992, but published in English by No Exit Press in 1994. The last Arjouni, *Brother Kemal*, was written with the author all too aware that he was under sentence of death. That book was also published in the UK in 2013 by No Exit Press, long champions of the author's work. While highly individual with a markedly cosmopolitan character, there are echoes in Arjouni's work of two of his literary heroes, Georges Simenon and Raymond Chandler, but the author was able to use the classic private eye novel to examine modern German society unflinchingly. He dealt provocatively with such issues as the Balkan wars and (in *One Man, One Murder*, 1992/2013), sex trafficking. Other issues explored in his sometimes incendiary body of work included religious intolerance.

The last book, *Brother Kemal*, translated by the much-respected Anthea Bell, has Kemal protecting an author at the Frankfurt Book Fair whose death has been decreed in a fatwa. Arjouni's own response to such theocratic brutality is made eloquently clear. Valerie de Chavannes, a financier's daughter, summons Kemal to her villa in Frankfurt's diplomatic quarter and commissions him to find her missing sixteen-year-old daughter Marieke. She is alleged to be with an older man who is posing as an artist. To Kayankaya, it seems like a simple case: an upper class girl with a thirst for adventure. Then another case turns up. The Maier Publishing House believes it needs to protect author Malik Rashid from attacks by religious fanatics at the Frankfurt Book Fair. Rashid has written a novel about, amongst other things, attitudes towards homosexuality in an Arabic country. Kayankaya is hired to be Rashid's bodyguard for three days. The two cases seem to be straightforward, but together they lead to murder, rape and abduction, and Kayankaya even comes under suspicion of being a contract killer for hire.

The many translations he enjoyed in his lifetime (not to mention the variety of literary prizes) were appropriate acknowledgements of a remarkable achievement in a very short life.

Saving the World

When a writer dies too young one remembers conversations – never to be repeated. I learnt the following when talking to the writer around the time of the UK issue of *Chez Max* – and now wish I'd spent more time talking to him. I asked Arjouni about inspirations. 'Well, frankly, I was inspired by some very diverse writers,' he told me. 'Dashiell Hammett, Georg Büchner, Heinrich Heine, Victor Hugo, William Faulkner, Guy de Maupassant, Eric Ambler, Samuel Beckett. Eclectic enough for you?' he said, smiling. However for *Chez Max*, he had two specific inspirations. 'For that book, it was Mark Twain and Jim Thompson. How about that for an ill-matched duo?'

'However, I am not a crime reader or, for that matter, a crime writer. I read books I like or love and sometimes these are crime stories. (For example, I consider Charles Willeford indispensable.) As a writer, if I think the story or a character I want to write about works best in the frame of a crime story, then this is the frame I use.' I asked how Arjouni felt a modern writer should tackle the thorny subject of sex. 'Hmmm... regarding sex and sexuality... I don't know what a contemporary writer should do or should not do. But as a writer you always try to find truth, don't you? Sometimes you find it with frankness, sometimes with discretion. I don't think that there are any simple rules to follow... with every page, every scene you have to find the words that work for this particular page or scene. During the actual work of writing, I work only for myself, not some notional reader. Writing is, de facto, communication. First, communication with myself and then, in a less direct way, communication with the world.'

He continued: '*Chez Max* plays in the future, 2064, in Paris. The planet is divided into the first and the second world, rich and poor, separated by a wall. The first world is democratic; people ride around on bicycles and eat good food. The second world is shadier, because the story is told from the wealthy perspective, but we hear about fanaticism, civil wars, dictators, terrorism, etc. The protagonist, Max Schwarzwald, lives in Paris, owns a gourmet restaurant and works part time for a government secret service. The principle of the service is: stop the criminals before they can execute their crimes. Max's partner in the secret service is Chen Wu, who (Max decides) is an arrogant, mean-spirited bigmouth. Max begins to suspect that Chen is helping illegal immigrants from the second world to come over the wall. Is Chen a member of a second world movement, some political underground party, perhaps even a terrorist group? So Max has to take things into his own hands… he has to save the world.'

Max Landorff: Confronting the Past

Translated by Baida Dar, Max Landorff's *Tretjak* (2013), already a bestseller in the German territories, is a tautly written psychological thriller set in Munich and around the Italian lakes. The eponymous Gabriel Tretjak is the Fixer, hired to play the part of fate in the lives of the rich and famous, to make the impossible possible. With clinical precision he rebuilds his clients' lives, no matter how murky their pasts. But a series of grisly murders soon threatens to destroy the life Tretjak has built for himself. The body of a famous brain surgeon is discovered in a horsebox; his eyes have been gouged out. The murderer leaves behind a series of tantalising clues – clues that all point to Tretjak. As the death toll rises and police suspicions mount, it dawns on Tretjak that he must confront the psychological puzzle of his own past if he is to survive. It's a trenchantly written piece, told in cool, disaffected style. This first novel by pseudonymous 'Max Landorff' is believed to be the work of the journalists and brothers Stephan and Andreas Lebert, since the novel was originally announced to the book trade under their name. The original German edition sold over 100,000 copies and spent weeks on the bestseller lists – a feat matched by its sequel, *The Hour of the Fixer*. The marketing campaign also meant that the book caused a stir even before its release: in an alternate reality game entitled 'Play the player, not the cards', the main character was brought to life, and players could enter into the world of 'the fixer', and become immersed in the events that developed around them, blurring the boundaries between fact and fiction. The campaign was so successful in building a fan base for the book that it won a silver award for marketing at the Leipzig Book Fair.

Paulus Hochgatterer: The Sweetness of Life

Should psychological thrillers play by the rules? Surely the best entries in the field achieve their effects by staying within certain parameters? There must be strongly developed central characters (with whom we identify), taking a journey into the darkest reaches of the human psyche, all with a persuasive leavening of psychological detail. Paulus Hochgatterer – who has a parallel career as a child therapist in Vienna – seems to have carved out a literary career by breaking (or at the very least, bending) the rules – empathy with his protagonists is kept on a tight leash. But this quaintly named author has proved with two highly distinctive books that it can be profitable to throw received wisdom out of the window.

Hochgatterer's *The Sweetness of Life* (2008, translated by Jamie Bulloch) was the Austrian recipient of a European prize for literature, and marked Hochgatterer out as a writer prepared to employ unorthodox effects. With a cast of troubled individuals in a village in Austria, the author detonated a series of literary incendiary devices following the discovery by a traumatised young girl of the mutilated body of her grandfather. Detective Superintendent Ludwig Kovacs joined sensitive psychiatrist Rafael Horn to open a particularly nasty can of worms. The book encountered some criticism for its dyspeptic vision of Austrian village life, but events in the real world have proved that (if anything) Hochgatterer underplayed the horrors that can lurk beneath the placid bourgeois surfaces.

The Sweetness of Life employed a variety of perspectives and narrators in what seemed like a determined attempt to avoid linear development. The same method is employed in *The Mattress House* (2012), and those in tune with the author's fragmented approach will find rich rewards. The divorced Kovacs is saddled with the well-worn accoutrements of the literary copper (including the now all too familiar difficulties of relating to a daughter), but contrasts satisfyingly with the psychiatrist Horn, who has his own problems. The Austrian retreat of Furth Am See sports a collection of damaged, mentally disturbed individuals. A young man dies after a fall from scaffolding, with foul play suspected. Then a rash of children, all bearing signs of abuse, comes to the attention of the police. The town is in turmoil, but Kovacs is unable to break through the wall of silence that the children have put up. There is a not-so-hidden agenda here: a provocative engagement with the rights and wrongs of the physical punishment of children. But Hochgatterer never forgets that his most urgent imperative is to deliver another forceful novel, moving to a gruesome conclusion. He may not care too much for careful narrative structure, but perhaps that's just why his unsettling books read like those of no other contemporary author.

Bernhard Schlink: Self-Deception

It's always pleasurable to make a new discovery in the crime fiction field (sometimes even more so if one can share it with like-minded readers), and for many readers, Bernhard Schlink's canny protagonist Gerhardt Self is an acquaintance they will be pleased to make. In the ingenious *Self-Deception*, the daughter of an important businessman has gone missing, and private detective Gerhardt Self is hired to track her down, leading him to encounter some dark doings in a secluded psychiatric hospital. Bernhard Schlink's seen-it-all private detective is shown to best advantage in this third book in the series. Self was a public prosecutor during the Third Reich, and is now a private investigator. He is a man at ease with himself, despite being nearly seven decades old and having a pretty dyspeptic view of the world, not least because of his past. And Germany's history – with its desperate moral convolutions – is always at the shadowed heart of the books.

Alexander Lernet-Holenia: Tales from the Vienna Woods

I Was Jack Mortimer (as translated from the German by Ignat Avsey) is a remarkable novel by Alexander Lernet-Holenia which has proved repeatedly attractive to filmmakers. A man climbs into Ferdinand Sponer's cab, gives the name of a hotel, and before he reaches it has been murdered: shot through the throat. And though Sponer has so far committed no crime, he is drawn into the late Jack Mortimer's life, and might not be able to escape its tangles and intrigues before it is too late. Twice filmed, but published belatedly in English in 2013, Holenia's novel is a tale of misappropriated identity as intricate and sonorous as the work of Patricia Highsmith. Its not-quite-innocent protagonist is consummately characterised, although the platinum-blonde femme fatale is perhaps more generic. *I Was Jack Mortimer* is also a book that evokes a Vienna in transition: from the glittering capital of the old aristocratic Austro-Hungarian empire to a shadier, altogether more prosaically modern city.

Ferdinand von Schirach:
Different in So Many Ways

I spoke to the German-born, UK-resident editor Stefanie Bierwirth, who has worked on crime titles both at Macmillan and Penguin. Surprise is a key element in the books she looks for. 'As with everything in life', she said, 'I think it is incredibly important to always be stimulated by new ideas and perspectives. Particularly in crime fiction, which is an area where readers constantly hunger for moments of surprise and want to solve unique puzzles that they haven't come across before. I've always felt that European crime fiction opens that canvas for crime and thriller fiction, and introduces its fans to new plots, moods and different ways of thinking. The increase in translated crime fiction and the general demand for foreign fiction – also on the big and small screen – proves that there is hunger for more all the time and discovering new novels in this area is an incredibly satisfying and stimulating process.

'As an editor in the area of crime in translation, but also as a native German speaker, I had great pleasure in taking on the English language rights to Ferdinand von Schirach's *The Collini Case* which is exactly one of those novels that is quintessentially different in so many ways. Of course, first and foremost this is a thrilling contemporary court case drama. But then on another level this novel also presents us with a very different story which I think strongly articulates the fact that we Germans are finally finding a different way of talking about our past and its legacy today. The reader, therefore, gets a richer, more complex experience.'

Jürgen Ehlers: No Conventional Hero

Jürgen Ehlers published his first crime piece *Flucht* (*Escape*) in 1992. Since then, numerous other short stories have appeared in anthologies and journals, nine of them in English. For his story *Weltspartag in Hamminkeln* (*World Savings Day in Hamminkeln*), Ehlers was awarded the Friedrich Glauser Prize in 2005. More recently, he has been tackling historical crime fiction: to date, five novels focussing on police detective Wilhelm Berger (and his family) have appeared, covering the period from 1917 to 1965. The Berger novels have been applauded as a commentary on German reality at particular periods in history. Ehlers' dark and wry short fiction may be set against his novels, which are based on authentic crimes. The first of these novels, *Mitgegangen*, was shortlisted as best debut novel by the 'Syndikat', the German crime writers' association. In *In Deinem schönen Leibe*, set in 1938, Berger and his colleagues try to crack the case of a missing girl. Has she fallen victim to a sadistic child killer? Berger is no conventional hero – he is a sceptical but basically apolitical citizen whose main concern is to protect his family. Under mounting pressure from his superiors, Berger finds it increasingly difficult to steer clear of the new political reality. State authority gains momentum, SA stormtroopers pay a visit to Berger's house, and his Jewish daughter by marriage hides a defector from the International Brigades under his roof. Anti-Semitic hatred explodes, and Berger's pre-Nazi middle-class world collapses around him.

Dupin Redux: but not Poe's Detective

The pseudonymous **Jean-Luc Bannalec** divides his time between his native Germany and the southern Finistère, and his books feature a detective who shares a name (but not much else) with Poe's creation Chevalier Dupin. *Bretonische Verhältnisse*, the first case for Commissaire Georges Dupin, was published in German in 2012. *Death in Pont-Aven* is targeted at the Donna Leon and Andrea Camilleri market. A bestseller in Germany, reaching number two on the *Der Spiegel* chart, selling over half a million copies in Europe and with a TV movie based on the book, this is a crime series to watch. Amiable and sun-drenched, the novel follows Dupin, a cantankerous, Parisian-born caffeine junkie, who is dragged from his morning croissants and coffee to the scene of a curious murder. The local village of Pont-Aven – a sleepy community by the sea where everyone knows one another and nothing much seems to happen – is in shock. The manager at the Central Hotel has come downstairs that morning to find ninety-one-year-old owner Pierre-Louis Pennec dead on the restaurant floor. Dupin and his team identify five principal suspects, including a rising political star, a longtime friend of the victim and a wealthy art historian. Further incidents – first a break-in, then another death – only compound the mystery. As Commissaire Dupin delves further and further into the lives of the victims and the suspects, he uncovers a web of secrecy and silence that belies the village's idyllic image. The novel's laidback, gentle appeal lies in Dupin's quirky methods and lifestyle, which include sea air and a Montalbano-like indulgence in fine wine and cuisine.

The German and Austrian Crime Screen

Out of the Shadow of the Reich: German Crime Films

There is a louring shadow over German crime cinema, and it is not just that of the grim days of the war. It is that of an autocratic director – one of the most influential in the history of the cinema, the brilliant (if bullying) Fritz Lang. Lang's iconic early crime films such as *M* (with its star-making turn as a child murderer by Peter Lorre) and the proto-Bond-villain *Dr Mabuse* (a character he was to make films about for several decades – the last was *The 1,000 Eyes of Dr Mabuse* in 1960) were the nihilistic blueprints for the doom-laden noir of American cinema. Ironically, the efforts by Goebbels to persuade Lang to become the Reich's film maestro precipitated the director's move to America where his re-definition of Expressionist crime film continued with such films as the brutal classic *The Big Heat*. Lang's four Mabuse films are an instructive index of crime film preoccupations over the years. The first silent Mabuse films were in the style of such outrageously eventful pulp serials as *Judex* and *Fantomas*, but by the sound era and *The Testament of Dr Mabuse* (1933), Lang was reflecting (and/or defining) such edgy American themes as government corruption and conspiracy. With his revisiting of his megalomaniac character in 1960, Lang transformed the espionage thriller with *The 1,000 Eyes of Dr Mabuse*, channelling notions of technologically-embedded terrorism, endemic surveillance and autocratic government.

Later filmmakers such as Ulli Lommel refined and re-invented the crime genre in such films as his serial killer movie made with a Douglas Sirk sensibility, *The Tenderness of Wolves*, while the parameters of violence (or more precisely, menace) were pushed further by Michael Haneke's extreme arthouse movies such as *Funny Games*. While Haneke is perhaps the most acclaimed German filmmaker of the early twenty-first century, his work does not represent the whole of modern German crime cinema, which also includes remarkable films such as *Run, Lola, Run* and *The Lives of Others*.

Selected Films (by date)

M (Film, 1931, Fritz Lang, director)

Fritz Lang's masterpiece remains as visually startling, clammy and unsettling as ever, and Peter Lorre's disturbing performance as a child murderer seems uncannily prescient in an age in which child abuse and molestation seem virtually quotidian. Some of the techniques forged by Lang here are still influential today. It is interesting, though, to compare the original to Joseph Losey's re-make, with David Wayne – until recently seemingly a lost film. Perhaps its touchy subject matter was the reason for its invisibility (as with Hammer's once-unseeable, now available *Never Take Sweets from a Stranger*?).

The Testament of Dr Mabuse (Film, 1933, Fritz Lang, director)

Lang's sinister classic now looks like a blueprint for much crime and thriller cinema that followed, with its all-seeing super villain using technology and surveillance in now-familiar fashion. Since the Nazis banned the film (sensing what the director was indirectly saying about the evil of the Reich), its reputation as a classic of German cinema has been unassailable.

Run, Lola, Run (Film, 1999, Tom Tykwer, director)

A young woman, the eponymous Lola, receives a phone call from her boyfriend telling her that he has left a bag containing 100,000 Deutschmarks on the subway which has been stolen by a homeless man. He has, however, to deliver the loot to ruthless criminal associates or suffer the consequences. His plan: rob a bank. Lola's plan: find the money (in whatever way she can) in the shortest possible time. In other words: run, Lola, run. This brief, intriguing and innovative film plays with real and screen time, conflating the two. We are shown the action in three 20 minute segments, each different from its predecessor. As well as being postmodern in its examination of the very nature of film, Tom Tykwer's film marries energy to keen intelligence.

The Lives of Others (Film, 2006, Florian Henckel von Donnersmarck, director)

The legacy of the past hangs heavily over *The Lives of Others*, an art film which enjoyed almost unprecedented (and almost populist) levels of exposure. Its seriousness of intent is signalled from the start (the film's subject is the distortion of life brought about under the brutal Stasi police force, with its 90,000 personnel), and performances are exemplary, notably that of the late Sebastian Koch as Dreyman, an East German socialist playwright who has persuaded himself that he has made an accommodation with the inhumane regime. Dreyman is careful to grind no ideological axe, and he maintains a studied political neutrality – although the fact that he has received state honours suggests that he cannot really claim any distance from the regime. But despite the collaborationist nature of his behaviour, he is not corrupt, and performs humane acts by intervening to save dissidents, including his friend Paul, a journalist. But he is to learn that attempting to finesse a totalitarian regime can have a heavy price. While utilising the apparatus of the thriller, this is nevertheless a film which has much to say about the problems of taking a moral stance in the face of institutional evil.

The Silence (Film, 2010, Baran bo Odar, director)
The fact that Baran bo Odar's unhurried but mesmeric film (like Jan Costin Wagner's original novel) shares a title with one of the director Ingmar Bergman's later classics is perhaps apposite. Like the Swedish filmmaker's censor-baiting uncompromising study of sexual alienation, this is a film which is prepared to unspool at precisely the pace that the director intends, with everything (from acting to *mise en scène*) treated with a rigour rare in arthouse cinema, let alone in a crime narrative such as this. As in the novel, the squabbling investigators move ever closer to a resolution of a rape and murder stretching over decades – but the audience is party to the identity of the killers as the initial crime is the sequence that opens the film. Apart from the sheer physical beauty of the film (at odds with the dark, twisted psychology of the characters presented) we're given the picture of a backwards-looking suburban town (the action here is transposed to Germany from the Finland of the original novel), and after the initial sexual assault and brutal killing with a rock of a young girl in a field of wheat, we are taken on a journey as disturbing as it is mystifying. If, perhaps, a particularly important plot twist is a touch unlikely, it is so authoritatively handled here that few will have cause to complain. Particularly vividly drawn is the sociopathic, barely-functioning hero, devastated by the death of his wife, who is nevertheless able to put clues together in the face of the intransigence of his colleagues. In terms of its structure, the film (looked at today) strikingly anticipates some of the Danish crime thrillers which were to follow.

SPAIN AND PORTUGAL

Iberian Bloodshed

The crime fiction of the Iberian Peninsula (Spain and Portugal) has acquired a distinctive character over the decades, fashioning sometimes quirky variations on the standard police procedural format. The local approach to the genre might be said to have had its gestation in the nineteenth century, but peninsular crime fiction achieved one of its most characteristic developments in what was dubbed the 'novela negra' movement of the 1970s (see Antonio Hill's comment below). The key authorial name in this era was **Manuel Vázquez Montalbán**, whose examination of socio-political aspects of his society added a considerable gravitas and commitment to the crime fiction form. Subsequent developments included a marked feminist perspective in crime novels of the 1980s and 1990s while Catalan and Basque strands in the genre addressed issues of regional nationalism.

The growth in Spanish crime talent has been propelled by such idiosyncratic and highly influential writers as Montalban and **Domingo Villar**, but emblematic of the genre's current rude health (although relatively few writers work within it) is the talented **Antonio Hill**, whose highly individual work is discussed below. I always enjoy meeting the ebullient, irrepressible Toni for meals in London and at crime panels in Harrogate. Iconoclastic conversations with him about his country's crime fiction (and not just his own), not to mention about Spain itself, are always highly illuminating.

'Spanish crime authors, as a breed, are not exactly thick on the ground', he told me. 'Or at least not so many that could legitimately be called "crime" authors from an Anglo-Saxon point of view. Let me elaborate a little bit: perhaps due to certain prejudices against crime novels (psychological thrillers and especially police procedurals), what you call "crime" in England is called in Spain "novela negra" (a version of the French idea of "noir"). The result is that many "noir" authors here approach the genre from a social perspective: many stories about losers, "marginals", etc. And most of them are written in a style that pretends to be – and sometimes is – more self-consciously literary than the usual standard. I am not saying that crime novels cannot be stylishly written, but I bet you know what I mean! And most of them have only reluctantly accepted the idea of being filed under the label of "noir" recently; significantly, after the phenomenal success of Stieg Larsson's books. Of course all these prejudices are being eroded, and in a few years there will probably be more authors prepared to be perceived as writers of pure crime fiction. In fact, there are some new names who don't feel self-conscious at all defending the once-undervalued "crime" genre.

'Crime fiction in Spain must be seen from a different perspective than in other European countries or in North America. Franco's dictatorship – which lasted, remember, for almost 40 years, from 1939–1975 – made it very difficult to write fiction with crime elements. Why? Well, perhaps for reasons that had to do with a national concept of morality and also – let's face it – with the unlikely choice (in that era) of a policeman as a hero. Back then, the police and army were loyal forces, symbols of the dictator and the totalitarian establishment, and they worked, especially in the 1940s and 1950s, as ruthless repressors, putting down any hint of rebellion against the government. Of course, nobody could write about their methods which routinely included torture, beatings, etc. The mere mention in any narrative of police corruption, so endemic in US noir from Chandler and Hammett onwards, or suggestions that social differences could cause or even justify (at least psychologically) any sort of crime, was unthinkable. The prevailing notion had to be like Stalin's Russia or today's North Korea: "Spanish people were all blissfully happy, and criminals were aberrations, bad guys who had to be deservedly punished by the all-knowing state." All novels (and films) from Spain – or foreign films we saw – had to be filleted by draconian censorship, moral guardians from some government office or the Catholic Church (perfect arbiters, of course, of what the rest of us should see or hear) who stamped the product as "good" or "bad", erased offending paragraphs from novels and cut any but the most anodyne scenes in movies. It was a dark time.'

Manuel Vázquez Montalbán: Communism and Kennedy

Manuel Vázquez Montalbán (1939–2003) is probably the most well-known Spanish crime writer abroad. His protagonist, Pepe Carvalho, is an ex-member of the Communist Party and also (ironically) an agent of the CIA. A disillusioned figure and a gastronome, his first appearance was in the novel *Yo maté a Kennedy/I Killed Kennedy* in 1972, in which he was a bodyguard, but Montalbán really found his form with *Tatuaje/Tattoo*, published two years later, a book which was the result of a bet between the author and some friends. Montalbán opined that he could write a crime novel in two weeks – which he proceeded to do. The author's books have been translated into 24 languages and reflect acutely the period of the Spanish transition from dictatorship to democracy. 'For me', Antonio Hill told me, 'the two finest are the Barcelona-set *Galindez* (1992) and *La soledad del manager/The Loneliness of the Manager* (2000)'. A favourite of British readers is *Murder in the Central Committee* (1981).

Francisco González Ledesma: Cut and Censored

Francisco González Ledesma is a classic case of an important author frustrated by censorship. At the age of 21 he received an important award (given by a jury that included no less than Somerset Maugham) for his novel *Sombras viejas/Old Shadows*. The book was not published when censorship bodies labelled Ledesma as a 'communist' and 'pornographer', which forced him to stop writing for a while, at least under his own name. Before the award, he had inaugurated another career, writing western and mystery novels under the pseudonym 'Silver Kane', delivering one novel a week, published in what would now be called pocket editions and sold in newsagents only. His output was staggering; Ledesma wrote about 300 novels. Finally, in the 1980s, his novel *Expediente Barcelona* was published in France by Gallimard. The writer had a huge success there – bigger, in fact, than in Spain. His crime novels feature Inspector Ricardo Méndez and are typical police procedurals. Despite his considerable age and poor health, Ledesma published a novel in 2013, although it may be his last – *Peores maneras de morir/Worse ways to Die*. All of his Mendez novels are set in Barcelona.

Andreu Martín was born in1949. Antonio Hill told me that Martin is one of his own favourite Spanish crime writers. He has tackled very different kinds of novels, some for young readers, and other more astringent books for adults. One of his finest novels is *Prótesis/Prothesis*, written in 1980. Martin is still actively writing and more recently has produced *Cabaret Pompeya* (a beguiling novel set in Barcelona in the years 1920–1975) and the tense *Sociedad Negra/Black Society* about a Chinese mob in Barcelona.

Born two years before Martin, **Juan Madrid** was strongly influenced by Chandler, Hammett and co., and sets his novels in the Madrid of the 80s. His series features Toni Romano, an ex-boxer and ex-policeman, who is something of a loser, but who undertakes investigations while he works for a company specialised in forcing debtors to pay what they owe. What may be his best novel does not belong to the series: *Días contados/Numbered Days* (1993) concerns a photographer in the Madrid of the 90s, where drugs have decisively ended the halcyon period of the 1980s. It is a tough love story and an unsparing social portrait of marginality.

Three other Spanish authors deserve mention: **Alicia Giménez Bartlett** (born 1951) is the creator of the first important female fiction character in Spanish crime: Inspector Petra Delicado. Bartlett has had a great success, and even gleaned the Raymond Chandler award (as did Manuel Vázquez Montalbán); she has published nine novels with her signature character, from the first, *Ritos de muerte/Death Rites* in 1996 to 2013's *Nadie quiere saber/Nobody Wants to Know*. **Lorenzo Silva**, who was born in 1966, has produced an important and heralded series, with Guardia Civiles Sergeant Rubén Bevilacqua and his loyal colleague, Virginia Chamorro. The first novel, *El lejano país de los estanques/The Remote Country of Lakes*, was published in 1998. *La marca del meridian/The Meridian Mark*, published in 2013, received the Planeta award, worth an impressive 600,000 euros. Both writers produce more or less classical police procedurals, and both also write other novels that have nothing to do with crime. Both also live in Barcelona and their novels are set in that city. **Domingo Villar**, born in 1971, established his status as one of the most challenging of Spanish authors of crime fiction with two significant novels set in Galicia,. His protagonist, Inspector Leo Caldas, has become a favourite of both critics and readers, with the novels *Ojos de agua/Water-Blue Eyes* and *La playa de los ahogados/The Beach of the Drowned*. Villar is a radio food critic and frequent contributor to various periodicals and he has also written scripts for film and television. *Water-Blue Eyes* won both the Brigada 21 Prize for best first crime novel as well as the Sintagma Prize. The novel, translated from the Spanish by Martin Schifino is rich in atmosphere. Amid the aroma of the sea and the Galician pines, a young saxophonist is found dead in his swanky flat overlooking the beach. The murder seems to have taken place after a sexual encounter with a lover: there are two glasses filled with gin in the living room, and the dead man, Luis Reigosa, is tied by the wrists to the headboard of the bed. But the way he was killed makes it impossible to obtain any more clues about his activities that night: his stomach, groin and thighs are horribly burned, and his genitals look hideously like a toasted cashew. The unusually cold-blooded and cruel murder is assigned to Leo Caldas, a disheartened police inspector still searching for his place in the world. The case unfolds between inviting nights at the jazz clubs and the tense, affected atmosphere of affluent Vigo.

Antonio Hill: A Spanish Explosion

According to Antonio Hill, Spain is currently experiencing an explosion of crime writers. (He describes this as the post-Larsson effect.) He is, of course, *primus inter pares* in this company. 'I am not sure why I decided to start writing a few years ago,' he told me. 'I was born in 1966, so I could have begun earlier, but I was sure I wanted to write crime fiction. I located my policeman in the Mossos d'Esquadra, the autonomical (regional) police force in Catalonia. I'm pleased to say that *The Summer of Dead Toys* became a best-seller in Spain, selling 100,000 copies, with publishing rights sold to 19 countries. The second book, *The Good Suicides*, has done well too, although the recession has affected sales, and the third – not exactly the last, but a sort of pause in the Hector Salgado series – is to be called *Los amantes de Hiroshima/The Lovers of Hiroshima*.'

My own admiration for Antonio Hill's work was forged by a reading of *The Summer of Dead Toys*. A stifling summer's morning in Barcelona. Inspector Hector Salgado has been lying awake, unable to sleep. He has just returned from Buenos Aires and is not in the best of moods – Salgado has lost his suitcase at the airport, and is deeply depressed after a painful separation from his wife and son. What's more, he is still recovering after having been brutally beaten by a suspect in a case he was involved in. The investigation had touched upon two incendiary subjects: paedophile rings and voodoo worshippers. But the beleaguered policeman's enforced leave of absence – during which his sympathetic boss is attempting to salvage Salgado's faltering career after the latter's own violent behaviour – is not to bring him peace. In order to take his mind off the case, his boss asks him to undertake an unofficial investigation into the circumstances behind the death of a student. But things are to get even worse for the embittered Spanish copper...

The first thing that strikes the reader about Antonio Hill's strikingly impressive debut novel is its evocative and atmospheric use of language (as rendered in Laura McGloughlin's nuanced translation). The sense of oppressive heat as the vulnerable Salgado muses on the mess his life is in is ever present, and the treatment of the sultry, louring city evokes the master of Barcelona-set narrative, Carlos Ruiz Zafon, in his novels *The Angel Game* and *The Shadow of the Wind*. But unlike those books, Hill's novel (despite its literary apparel) is a crime story, and the author – whose other speciality is psychology – seems to have arrived fully formed with confidence and authority, peeling back the skeins of deceit and betrayal in the most satisfying of fashions. His detective (like so many of his predecessors) is to uncover layers of corruption in the upper echelons of Barcelona society, as a teenager's fall to his death leads to the unveiling of clandestine truths involving two of the city's most influential families. Hill clearly knows his genre fiction, and utilises one of the most shopworn (but comforting) conventions of the crime field: two initially unrelated cases that are to be linked by a detective at the end of his tether, at some cost to the investigator. But for all the storytelling skills Antonio Hill displays in *The Summer of Dead Toys*, his real achievement here is in the creation of an idiosyncratic and edgy new series character. Hector Salgado, one suspects, may be put together from a variety of familiar elements plucked magpie-style from other writers, but he emerges (finally) as something keenly individual. As Hill shows every sign of keeping up the momentum of his inaugural effort, this is a series to watch.

Eugenio Fuentes: At Close Quarters

Eugenio Fuentes was born in Montehermoso, Cáceres, Spain in 1958 and currently lives in Extremadura. He is a multi-prize-winning writer of five novels and a short-story collection, and a writer of distinction. His work has been translated into more than thirteen languages, and lays bare a clandestine Spain. *At Close Quarters* (translated by Martin Schifino) is typically involving. Every day Samuel watches as a woman drops off her two children at the bus stop. He is so fascinated by her that, one afternoon when he cannot be at his window to observe her, he leaves his camera programmed to take pictures of her picking up the children. Later, when he looks through the pictures, he sees an unexpected event that has been photographed. That day, on the corner, a group of teenagers provokes one of the neighbour's dogs, which ends up killing one of them. Samuel decides to approach the woman. Her name is Marina, she is recently separated, and the daughter of a high-ranking officer, Captain Olmedo, who was in charge of dismantling the city's military headquarters, and who is found dead in his house, with a bullet from his own gun through his chest. His daughter does not believe the official version of the suicide and she hires Cupido, a peaceful detective who will discover hidden secrets as well as the tense relationships of those who surround them.

The same translator has capably rendered *The Pianist's Hands*, sporting a topical theme. As in so many cities in the heat of growth, Breda, Spain, is home to a modest construction company that wants to take advantage of the booming times to construct a luxury housing-complex in the suburbs. Although between the business partners there are differences of opinion and fears about such an ambitious project, expectation of its sumptuous benefits pushes them to go through with the scheme. Then the corpse of one of the partners appears inside one of the newly constructed buildings. Detective Ricardo Cupido delves into a passionate investigation where the alibis matter less than the dark and desolate description of the human condition. Other novels include *Blood of the Angels* and *In the Depths of the Forest*, the latter translated by Paul Antill, and winner of the Alba/Prensa Canaria prize in 1999.

Luis Fernando Verissimo: Portuguese Espionage

It must have been one hell of a job. Translating *The Spies* into English from its native Portuguese will not have been easy. At first glance, this slim book might seem to be a mere *jeu d'esprit*: a lightweight, humorous novella with a touch of Borges which is also a kind of riff on the work of John le Carré – an author repeatedly namechecked in

Verissimo's book. The language may have given the excellent translator Margaret Jull Costa pause but she has risen to the challenge. Every word in the Portuguese original has been weighed, sampled and slotted into a perfectly constructed whole, and Costa's rendering – both lucid and deceptively simple – does satisfying justice to the book. That said, for all its accomplishment, this is not a book for every taste – not every reader will be able to discern its appeal.

The central character is a publisher whose attitude to his authors is distinctly cool, and his real pleasure comes not from working on the books he publishes but from pointless discussions with a quirky group of friends who gather at the Bar do Espanhol near his office. Desultory arguments – often repeated – focus on the place of the comma and the worthlessness (or genius) of famous authors. But Verissimo's protagonist is under no illusions about the usefulness of these debates. 'It was,' he says, 'a way of dramatising our own inescapable mediocrity, a kind of mutual flagellation through banality.' Of course, this group (who describe themselves as the living dead) are ripe for something to shake them out of their dull existence. That happens when the publisher receives a puzzling letter with a sample chapter. Ariadne, who lives in the secluded town of Frondosa, is considering suicide but one thing is delaying the act: she wants to complete the memoir she's working on. The narrator adopts the role of the spymaster in his beloved le Carré novels, sending out various friends to find out what's happening to this self-destructive woman. Of course, none of these emissaries proves up to the task of helping the mysterious Ariadne. There are many eccentric and memorable characterisations here, and the clever parody of the spy/detective story points up the latter's absurdities. But the wry, affectless prose will not be for every palate, and a cursory reading may make *The Spies* appear to be a very slight piece. But for those prepared to give themselves over to this unusual Brazilian writer, there is treasure hidden just underneath the surface.

A Portuguese Miscellany

Portugal has boasted its share of highly accomplished crime writers, with **José da Natividade Gaspar** furnishing several Golden Age detective novels and solid work from later writers such as **Francisco José Viegas** (with his eccentric copper Jaime Ramos), **Fernando Luso Soares** and the prolific, Anglocentric **Ana Teresa Pereira**.

Arturo Pérez-Reverte: Exuberance and Cynicism

The Siege (2013), translated by Frank Wynne, is a typical piece of exuberant Pérez-Reverte writing, with a perky line in modern cynicism freighted into its period narrative. Cádiz, 1811: Spain is battling for independence. But in the streets of the most liberal city in Europe other battles are taking place. A serial killer is on the loose, flaying young women to death. Each of these murders takes place near the site where a French bomb has just fallen. It is the job of policeman Rogelio Tizon to find the murderer and avoid public scandal in a city already poised on the brink. Cádiz is a complex chessboard on which an unseen hand is moving the pieces that will decide the fate of its protagonists: a corrupt and brutal policeman; the female heir to an important shipping company; an unscrupulous corsair captain; a taxidermist who is also a spy; a hardened soldier; and an eccentric French artilleryman. Stirred into this rich brew are the intrigue and energy of such earlier books as *The Dumas Club* and *The Flanders Panel*. *The Siege* is as much about a city shaken by violent change as it is about its disparate characters.

Teresa Solana: The Sound of One Hand Killing

If they're on Bitter Lemon Press's mailing list for launch invitations, London crime aficionados are sometimes lucky enough to meet at the publisher's bashes some of the best European crime writers at work today. And the company's urbane publisher François von Hurter also has a keen grasp of the crime fiction idiom as practised in non-Anglo Saxon countries. I asked him why he'd undertaken the risky step of becoming a respected foreign crime maven. 'The challenge is part of the pleasure,' he told me. 'And, for me, another of the main pleasures of publishing non-Scandinavian crime novels is that of rediscovering that humour is an essential ingredient of crime writing. Elmore Leonard led the way, and Carl Hiaasen followed. And two authors I've published, Tonino Benacquista and Teresa Solana. Or just think of the Coen brothers' *Fargo* or *Burn after Reading*, to bring in another medium. These authors – and these films – make you laugh out loud. But often a smile is reward enough; sadly, a rare reward if you stick to our brothers of the frozen North in print or even in their celebrated TV series. Can you remember smiling once as you dutifully watched all the episodes of *The Killing*?

'But you asked why I undertake the risky business of publishing translated crime. Here's one reason: the aforementioned Teresa Solana, an author of wonderful crime novels set in Barcelona, witty and brimming with malicious satire. She is translated by her husband, Peter Bush, which makes for an interesting dynamic. Peter is a very gifted literary translator but, as is often the case with the best in this field, he knows next to nothing about weapons. It's always a pleasure to correct passages that confuse pistols and revolvers, rounds and bullets, shells and cartridges. The murder weapon in the latest Solana was a statuette of the Buddha – so no problem there. But in Catalan the novel was called *L'Hora Zen – The Zen Hour*. This made sense as the world of alternative medicine was spoofed, describing a meditation centre called "L'Hora Zen" in the ritziest part of Barcelona. *The Zen Hour* sounded like a cross between a self-help book and a guide to "meditation lite". So we came up with *The Sound of One Hand Killing*.'

The Spanish and Portuguese Crime Screen

Call Girl (Film, 2007, António-Pedro Vasconcelos, director)

An ambitious crime thriller with a complex and multi-stranded take on political corruption. Prostitution is utilised as a flexible metaphor for the ethos of the serviceable and amoral characters. Director António-Pedro Vasconcelos is perhaps not able to keep all the strands in balance, but moulds with immense skill the performances of Soraia Chaves, Ivo Canelas and Nicolau Breyner.

Spanish Crime Film Musings

Two other crime films of note are *El crack/The Crack* made by José Luis Garcia in 1981: a classical noir with a sardonic private investigator and ex-policeman as protagonist, and *Fanny Pelopaja* (1984, by Vicente Aranda). A rough translation of the latter film's title might be something like *Fanny Straw-hair* and it is an uncompromising crime thriller focussing on a bent cop and his sadomasochistic relationship with the woman of the title. It is a (very) free adaptation of the novel *Prótesis* by Andreu Martin, an important Spanish writer.

GREECE

Under the pitiless sun, a lengthy tradition of Grecian crime and murder stretches back to the bloodletting of Greek tragedy and continues in the work of such novelists as Petros Markaris. Over the years, the Scottish-born crime writer Paul Johnston has proved to be one of the most protean practitioners in the field, the effortless master of a variety of genres. Many readers fondly remember his near-future thrillers featuring eccentric detective Quintilian Dalrymple. But given the author's long residence in Greece, it's hardly surprising that some of his finest writing has involved this sun-baked country. A good example is the recent *The Black Life*, a strongly written novel told in alternating chapters which sets present day Greece against the years of the Holocaust. Johnston's protagonist, half-Greek, half-Scottish private eye Alex Mavros, is the perfect conduit through the bifurcated narrative, which is as much an examination of Greek identity as it is of the horrors of the Second World War. The book is both truthful and (occasionally) excoriating about the writer's adopted country, but Greece is now clearly embedded in the DNA of this talented novelist. Which is why I asked Paul (never slow to voice an opinion) for a snapshot of *crime à la grecque*. He told me: 'Crime writing in modern Greece has a shorter history than in other European countries, but has made up for that in recent years. An interesting forerunner is *The Murderess* (1903) by **Alexandros Papadiamandis**, described by the author as "a social novel". It certainly is that – the main issue being the harsh lives of island women – but the story is also a meditation on crime and punishment and a skilful psychological analysis of the old woman, Frangoyiannou, who kills infant girls to save them from lives of toil. Papadiamandis is often seen as the Greek Dostoyevsky. Many late nineteenth and early twentieth century novels in the ethnographic tradition describe criminal activities, but usually at the familial and village level. It was only with the influx of over a million Greeks from Turkey in the early 1920s that industry and the urban conditions for crime fiction were established.

Such was the political control over the heavily policed pre-World War Two society that crime only really featured in the "rebetika" musical tradition, often compared with the blues in its concentration on the poor, the outcast and small-time criminals. Illicit love and drugs are often the subjects of songs, the instrumentation based on the plangent notes of bouzouki and baglamas.

'Post-war Greece saw the development of pulp crime fiction, available from pavement kiosks rather than bookshops. The undisputed godfather of Greek crime writing was **Yannis Maris** (pseudonym of the left-wing journalist Yannis Tsirimokos, 1916–79) who was the author of *The Man on the Train* (1958). Starting in 1953, he wrote over forty short and well-plotted novels that have only recently been accepted as classics of the genre. His detective, Inspector Bekas, became an institution and has inspired a contemporary TV series. Maris was also an inspiration for **Petros Markaris** (b. 1937), whose Inspector Haritos is the best known current fictional detective in Greece. His novels – such as *Zone Defence*, *The Late-Night News* and *Che Committed Suicide* – have been translated into English and numerous other continental languages. Haritos is an engaging character, devoted to his daughter, keen on his wife's cooking and a habitual reader of the dictionary, but also smart and dogged, if rather conventional. He has been accurately described as the Greek Maigret. More recently Markaris has written a trilogy about the Greek financial crisis. Numerous sacred cows are skewered and social concerns are to the fore. In Greece everything is political and Markaris's hugely popular works show how disillusioned people have become with the establishment.

'Greek crime fiction now attracts attention from serious publishers and reviewers – probably more so as regards the latter than in the UK. In 2010 the Greek Crime Writers' Club was set up and now has around 30 members. Much of their work is worthy of translation and covers many aspects of historical and modern Greece. While crime fiction was traditionally seen as a summer beach read, it now has year-round appeal. **Sergios Gakas** has written a fine example of Greek noir: his *Ashes* (2011) reeks of graft, violence and the need for revenge. And two literary novelists who use the tropes of crime fiction are also worthy of note: **Alexis Stamatis's** *Bar Flaubert* (2006) has a protagonist in search of himself via a mysterious manuscript; while **Ioanna Bourazopoulou's** *What Lot's Wife Saw* (2013), which won the Athens Prize for Literature, is a blend of, among other things, Thomas Pynchon and Agatha Christie. Finally, it is striking that a large amount of foreign crime fiction is translated into Greek. **Andreas Apostolides**, as well as producing excellent novels such as *Lobotomy*, 2002, has translated James Ellroy and numerous other writers. This means that readers of crime fiction in Greece are well informed about the genre internationally, and writers primed to adapt the best models to the local milieu.'

Petros Markaris: Foul Play

We should consider in more detail one of the novelists mentioned above by Paul Johnston. Petros Markaris was born in Istanbul in 1937 and lived in Athens, where he became Director of the National Book Centre of Greece. His bestsellers are published in 14 languages, with *The Late-Night News* and *Zone Defence* published in the UK by Harvill Secker, while *Che Committed Suicide* and *Basic Shareholder* were published by Arcadia Books. My ex-literary editor at the *Independent*, Boyd Tonkin, was fulsome in his praise. 'Markaris is no formula-bound hack,' he said, 'but a versatile author who, in his mysteries, turns the hero's sleuthing into a spotlight on a fast-changing Greek society.' *Che Committed Suicide*, translated from the Greek by David Connolly, is a contemporary crime novel, a book that examines the social fabric of Greece today, a country still very much at the top of the news agenda, although, perhaps, for all the wrong reasons. It's 30 years after the end of the military dictatorship, and former Junta-opponent Favieros is a successful man. His building company is flourishing and preparations for the 2004 Olympic Games are in full flow. What, then, has made him decide to shoot himself on live television in front of a million viewers? Nobody suspects foul play, with the exception of the methodical Inspector Costas Haritos, on medical leave, and looking for any excuse to relieve his boredom and to escape the suffocating atmosphere at home. The event awakens his curiosity, and propels him to launch his own investigation. Then, when two equally spectacular public suicides – of a politician and a famous journalist – take place, indifference turns to panic amongst the police, who have little to go on. Inspector Haritos is called upon to help unveil the secrets buried in the victims' past, and it seems that the key to the mystery is inextricably linked to the political scene in modern-day Greece, examined in nuance and intriguing fashion by Markaris.

Ioanna Bourazopoulou: What Lot's Wife Saw

Winner of the Athens Prize for Literature in 2008, the bizarre *What Lot's Wife Saw* (translated by Yiannis Panas) is set in a post-apocalyptic world, ruled by a mysterious business consortium where commerce has replaced belief: a modern day Sodom and Gomorrah. The book heralds an unusual talent in Ioanna Bourazopoulou who weaves a fabulist sensibility, crime tropes, sociopolitical critique and linguistic wordplay into a heady but surprisingly nourishing brew. It's been twenty-five years since the Overflow flooded Southern Europe, drowning Rome, Vienna and Istanbul, and turning Paris into a major port. At the Dead Sea, the earth has opened up to reveal a strange violet salt to which the world has become addicted, and a colony has been established by the mysterious Consortium of Seventy-Five to control the supply. Run by murderers, fugitives and liars, the Colony is a haven to those fleeing Europe, especially the privileged 'Purple Stars'. But when the governor of the Colony dies suddenly and mysteriously, the six officials turn on each other, sparking a terrifying chain of events. Tensions and old enmities are reignited as the leaderless officials battle each other, threatening the Colony's very existence. In Europe, Phileas Book, the greatest crossword compiler of his age and creator of the 'Epistleword', is recruited by the sinister Consortium. Presented with the epistolary confessions of the six, he is ordered to sift truth from lies. Who killed the unpopular Governor Bera? What happened in the Colony? And why is Phileas Book the only one who can solve the mystery?

What Lot's Wife Saw, occasionally incoherent, is still an iconoclastic, exuberantly written novel about the layers of guilt and regret that beset the human psyche. A massive bestseller in Greece, it is a darkly sardonic parable with an Old Testament morality at its heart.

THE NETHERLANDS

Rats, Nosferatu and Maarten 't Hart

Admired by no less a person than the formidable Patricia Highsmith, the unconventional writer Maarten 't Hart's novels sold in their hundreds of thousands in his native Holland, where he gained something of a reputation as a cross-dresser, often appearing on chat shows dressed as a female alter ego, 'Martha'. 't Hart is the author of over ten novels, and his work has been widely translated. His unusual interest in rats led the writer to assist the equally eccentric director Werner Herzog in his remake of *Nosferatu*, which featured 't Hart's verminous favourite animals.

The Sundial (translated from the Dutch by Michiel Horn) begins with Leonie Kuyper attending the funeral of her best friend Roos Berczy, who has seemingly died of sunstroke. Leonie has always felt somewhat overshadowed by Roos, who was striking looking and a brilliant pharmacological research assistant to boot. She turns out to have made Leonie her sole heir, provided that she moves into Roos's apartment and cares for her cats. For Leonie, an impoverished translator, it is an offer she cannot refuse and she becomes the owner of a beautiful apartment, a large portfolio of common stocks, and an expensive wardrobe. Gradually Leonie assumes Roos's identity. By wearing her clothes and make-up, she begins to resemble her deceased friend and, as a result, Roos's past starts to crowd in on her. Was Roos a chemist involved in the manufacture of Ecstasy? But Leonie is also confronted with the possibility that Roos had information about the falsification of research findings and might have been murdered by a colleague. *The Sundial* reflects the author's personal fascination with the nebulousness of identity, but counterpoints its eccentricity with genuine narrative rigour. Maarten 't Hart won the Golden Noose crime fiction award in 1994.

Dutch Detectives

One of the most popular features of the magazine I edit, *Crime Time*, has been the foreign 'crime scene' series edited by the crime fiction commentator Bob Cornwell, in which Bob draws on an unparalleled network of contacts, mainly from AIEP/IACW, the Association of International Crime Writers. One such is the writer and crime expert Charles den Tex, along with his colleague Jos van Cann. Their overview of the Netherlands in issue #56 is instructive, and Charles has been singularly helpful with the section you are reading now. His novels include *The Power of Mr Miller* and *CELL*, and he is a three-time winner of the Golden Noose, the leading Dutch prize for crime fiction. His work is discussed below.

Politics and conspiracies loom large in the writing of **Tomas Ross**, the grand old man of Dutch crime fiction. He was one of the founders of the Netherlands Association of Crime Fiction Writers. He published his first thriller in 1980 and has since published 53 more, winning the Golden Noose three times: in 1987 for *Bèta*, 1996 for *Koerier voor Sarajevo* (*Courier for Sarajevo*) and 2003 for *De zesde mei* (*May 6*). **René Appel** has been publishing since 1987. He has developed his own style in psychological thrillers and has won the Golden Noose twice: in 1991 for *De derde persoon* (*The Third Person*) and 2001 for *Zinloos geweld* (*Senseless Violence*). **Roel Janssen** made a niche for his writing with his financial thrillers, winning the Golden Noose in 2007 for *De tiende vrouw* (*The Tenth Woman*). **Elvin Post** has distinguished himself with his particular brand of bizarre thriller, winning the Golden Noose in 2004 for *Groene vrijdag* (*Green Friday*) and the Diamond Bullet in 2011 for *Room Service*. In 1985 **Ina Bouman** wrote the first of five books featuring her journalist heroine Jos Welling. That novel became identified as 'the first feminist thriller' in the Netherlands. In the 1990s Lydia Rood and her brother Niels wrote a series of seven police novels as **Rood & Rood**. And one should mention the immensely professional **Janwillem van de Wetering**.

Well-known to fans of translated crime (and highly thought of) is **A C Baantjer**, a former Amsterdam policeman who has written over seventy novels. His Inspector Dekok books are still highly popular, and were the basis for a long-running TV series. In 2003, Baantjer received the medal of honour from the GNM, the Dutch crime writers association. **Simon De Waal**, an Amsterdam serious crimes police inspector and screenwriter wrote *Cop vs Killer* which was filmed for television, and *Pentito* which won the Diamond Bullet, the Flemish annual crime fiction award, in 2008. He has successfully continued the Baantjer series under the name *De Waal En Baantjer*. **Corine Hartman** introduced female detective Jessica Haider, a hard-working, dope-using policewoman, and has won the Crimezone Thriller award twice: in 2011 for *Als de dood* (*Scared to Death*) and in 2013 for *Bloedlijn* (*Blood Line*). **Bert Muns**, himself a police detective, writes about a female inspector working in Utrecht. **Bert Spoelstra** chronicles the investigations of Ruud Haas, a popular series (not least with the police themselves), as well as another series about Hoonstra, a suspended detective with a dark personality. The prolific novelist and TV writer **Ed van Eeden**, known as 'Big Dutch', is the author of the *Dossier* series set in Utrecht.

Dutch Private Eyes and Other Hardboiled Fare

Gerben Hellinga, writing as **Hellinger**, made his debut in the 1960s with a series of four crime novels featuring Sid Stefan. He returned to the character in 1989, winning the Golden Noose with the first of the new series, *The Return of Sid Stefan*. Between 1980 and 2003, psychologist and crime critic **Theo Capel** penned ten offbeat private eye novels featuring Hank Stammer, an Amsterdam repo-man who is fond of country music. From 1980, the versatile **Felix Thijssen** wrote eight books featuring the amoral Charlie Mann. In 1998, he introduced Max Winter, a more conventional private eye, winning the Golden Noose 1999 for *Cleopatra*, the first of the series. **Peter de Zwaan's** noirish non-mainstream novels were nominated for the Golden Noose four times before finally winning in 2000 for *Het Alibibureau* (*The Alibi Bureau*). His novels also feature USA (Denver)-based private eye Jeff Meekes. **Escober**, the nom de plume of Esther and Berry Verhoef, has published five hard action thrillers, winning the Diamond Bullet in 2005 for *Onder druk* (*Under Pressure*).

The Literary Thriller

The formidable **Saskia Noort** is currently the bestselling *grande dame* of crime fiction in the Netherlands. She was awarded the Master Prize in 2013 for transforming the Dutch thriller market. Also selling well are the psychological thrillers of **Esther Verhoef**, once a writer on animal life, and now the female half of thriller team Escober. **Simone van der Vlugt**, with 12 thrillers to her name, is prolific and enormously successful. She won the Crimezone Thriller award in 2009 for *Blauw water* (*Blue Water*). In 2010 her book *Op klaarlichte dag* (*In Broad Daylight*) won both the Crimezone Thriller Award and the NS Publieksprijs.

Charles den Tex

He published his first thriller in 1995 and has subsequently published fifteen books, winning the prestigious Golden Noose three times: in 2002 for *Schijn van kans* (*Chance in Hell*), in 2006 for *De macht van meneer Miller* (*The Power of Mr Miller*) and two years later for *CELL*. His novel *De vriend* (*The Friend*) won the 2012 Crimezone Thriller award, and in 2013 he bagged another prize, the Gouden Vleermuis (*Golden Bat*) for his body of work. Den Tex is perhaps best known for his *Bellicher Trilogy* (*The Power of Mr Miller*, *CELL* and *Password*), featuring management consultant Michael Bellicher, immersed in conspiracies, identity theft and surveillance systems in an era in which internet technology and age-old crimes converge. *The Power of Mr Miller* and *CELL* were filmed as a ten-part television series.

Simone van der Vlugt: Safe as Houses

Dutch writer Simone van der Vlugt has written eight accomplished thrillers, and *Safe as Houses* (translated by Michele Hutchinson), which sold a million copies in Holland, is what her publishers proposed as her breakthrough book in the UK. Home is generally considered to be a safe place – but when a man forces his way into Lisa's house, taking both the parent and her young daughter hostage, what ensues is a particularly terrifying experience. What is most disturbing is the man's motivation. What does he want from Lisa? As the hours and days tick agonisingly past, she finds herself in a terrifying struggle to survive – and she cannot understand why the only witness to the attack has not raised an alarm. This may be perceived as psychological suspense, but that's not to ignore its frisson-producing effect as a piece of well-orchestrated thriller writing – and Simone van der Vlugt delivers exactly what the reader requires in this territory.

POLAND

Marek Krajewski: The End of the World in Breslau

The Polish author Marek Krajewski sets readers a knotty challenge in his rich and idiosyncratic Breslau novels. Atmosphere and piquant period detail positively saturate the pages, and push these books into the upper echelons of literary crime. But Krajewski's cynical, sybaritic Criminal Councillor Eberhard Mock – with his eternally unslaked appetites and cruel brutality to his beautiful wife Sophie – has the reader wondering: do we really want to spend time in the company of this unattractive protagonist? Krajewski, however, has second-guessed this possible objection. Mock, however unappealing, is not as off-putting as many of the characters he encounters in this privileged, decadent society, so we reluctantly accept him as our guide. *Death in Breslau* (2008) had critics scrabbling for superlatives, and *The End of the World in Breslau*, published in 2010, gleaned similar endorsements in Danusia Stok's pellucid translation. 1920s Breslau is a cornucopia of lowlife crime and aristocratic debauchery. Eberhard Mock, locked in a violent relationship with his young wife in a sumptuous mansion, is at home in this society, indulging in its vices with enthusiasm. The body of a man has been discovered bound and walled up alive, another has been dissected, his fingers chopped off. The victims have nothing in common – one is a locksmith, one a musician – but both are found with a calendar page with the date of their death marked in blood. Krajewski's caustic protagonist takes time off from his disintegrating marriage to plunge headlong into the bordellos, gambling joints and bathhouses of Breslau to track down a particularly savage murderer. Mock is hardly in a position to make too many moral judgements, but even he is given pause by a series of drug-fuelled aristocratic orgies that have been concealed by an ingenious use of hypnosis. Meanwhile, Sophie, chafing at the abuse from her husband, has initiated her own journey of sexual indulgence with her friend Elizabeth – and she comes into contact with a cryptic figure who is somehow feeding the apocalyptic fever sweeping 1920s Breslau.

Those exhausted by crime fiction set in the violent council estates of modern Britain will pounce on this ferocious odyssey into a lost world of decadence, class and deception. It's not a comfortable journey (particularly in the louche company of its anti-hero Mock), but Krajewski, as before, performs the key function of the skilful novelist: providing an *entrée* into a world so far from our own that the Breslau depicted here seems like some bizarre science fiction landscape. If you're looking for an evocation of a more comforting age in your historical crime fiction, you'd better steer well clear of the lacerating narratives of Marek Krajewski.

Severing the Minotaur's Head

Sometimes an author arrives sporting an utterly individual style that decisively marks them out from fellow writers; Krajewski is clearly in that august company. Discerning readers are discovering his work, which marries literary weight with sheer narrative nous. Krajewski's protagonist, Abwehr Captain Eberhard Mock, has long shown signs of becoming an essential travelling companion for many aficionados of crime in translation. *The Minotaur's Head* (2012, translated by Danusia Stock) might almost be said to function as a signature book, with all the writer's virtues shiningly in evidence. Breslau 1939. Eberhard Mock is summoned from a New Year's Eve party to a notably blood-boltered crime scene which gives even the hardened detective pause. A young girl (who has been suspected of espionage), recently arrived by train from France, is discovered murdered in a hotel room, the skin ripped from her cheek by the teeth of her murderer. In Poland, a series of equally horrific crimes in the same vein has the populace in terror. Mock makes the journey across the border to assist his colleague Commissioner Popielski (with whom he shares a taste for a sybaritic lifestyle and the pleasures of the mind), and this idiosyncratic duo is soon on the trail of a particularly grotesque killer. As in earlier books by Krajewski, it is hard to know what to praise first here: the pithily realised foreign locales, the subtly inflected sense of period or the Ancient Mariner-like storytelling grip. In the final analysis, though, it is probably the luxuriantly realised characterisation of the two slightly eccentric coppers that sounds the most piquant note; their interchanges are one of the particular pleasures of the book.

Zygmunt Miloszewski: Entanglement

The publisher Bitter Lemon has long been a barometer for the best crime fiction in translation, and that reputation was consolidated by *Entanglement*, a trenchant piece of crime writing from Poland. A monastery in Warsaw is the subject of an unforgiving therapy encounter. A man has been murdered, his eye socket transfixed by a roasting spit. Dogged State copper Teodor Szacki is handed the case, and finds he has his hands full with a colourful dramatis personae – not to mention an earlier murder several years ago, when communism was in full flower. This is flinty, quirky crime writing with a pungent sense of locale and a nicely jaded protagonist in Szacki, the past-his-sell-by-date copper energised by the case. Miloszewski is another interesting name for the Bitter Lemon stable.

ROMANIA

The publisher Profusion has been making available some extraordinary crime fiction novels from Romanian authors in English translation. *Attack in the Library* (*Atac în bibliotecă*) by **George Arion** introduced Andrei Mladin, a committed and public-spirited citizen whose hobbies are drinking and sex. He's also a counter-intuitive detective, inveigled in this book by a seductive blonde violinist who gets him in a web of deceit and murder. The CWA Silver Dagger winner, writer Mike Phillips, extolled its virtues:

'Arion's *Attack in the Library* is one of the classic narratives of Romanian popular fiction. Written during the dictatorship of the 1980s, it weaves a gripping narrative out of the bars, the housing estates and restaurants of Bucharest. Arion's characters queue for food, cope with power blackouts, sweat in the heat and struggle with the privileges and influence of the elites. Some critics have speculated that *Attack* escaped the attentions of official censorship because it was disguised as a humorous crime fiction romp. Whatever the truth of the matter, however, the novel was, in the circumstances, an almost suicidal act of daring. Publications which criticise the former regime are, nowadays, more or less, commonplace. Almost all of these have been published (if not written) during the last two decades, and written largely by authors who grew up in the West or who fled the country during the dictatorship. *Attack* is extraordinary because it emerges from the moment in which it was written, and the author was located, stubbornly, inside the circumstances he was observing. He speaks, therefore, with the authentic voice of a man in the street, and details the style and attitudes which made everyday life possible for ordinary Romanians. At the time, crime fiction publications in Romania were mainly "about" espionage, describing the exploits of government security men and the corruption of the West. Another strand imitated the country house mysteries of the tradition exemplified by Agatha Christie. *Attack* was a calculated lampoon of the "body in the library" tradition, but the novel went on to be a thoroughgoing and thoughtful critique of the regime. The mockery of the dictator and his cronies, however, is also a mask for an exploration of other aspects of the society. Unlike other significant critics of the regime, Arion describes the emergence of an entrepreneurial class, along with their potential for corruption and exploitation of the population, an experience which was also part of post-communist liberation. He writes, therefore, from "inside" the mind of the ordinary Romanian with everyday characters like the neighbourhood busybodies, the struggling militiamen, and the local drunks. He achieves this, partly, by his invention of a rich and innovative demotic, a language studded with and inspired by the street idioms and metaphors of his native Bucharest. Here again, Arion is a notable innovator. The regime and its institutions privileged the language and the style of the "classics". Arion's method, based on his journalistic experience and knowledge, pointed the way for a literature which could deal with everyday observations, as well as the changes and events in the landscape which surrounded him.'

Phillips, in fact, translated the book with Ramona Mitrica and Mihai Risnoveanu.

Finding the Right Idiom

I've also spoken to Mike Phillips (a considerable crime novelist in his own right, along with his multiplicity of other interests) about the challenges of translating European languages. His views, once expressed to me before a BBC radio programme we were doing on black crime writers, are typically trenchant:

'Conventional translators have traditionally struggled to locate, in English or American usage, equivalents for an author's idiomatic practices. This is, in any case, part of a network of strategies, designed to avoid the fundamental error of producing sentences which "translate" the literal meanings of words, while making no sense to an English reader. Nevertheless, the attempt to create fluent English versions all too often results in bland, characterless texts in which the relationship of the language to specific cultures and circumstances is completely lost. This raises another, different issue, to do with the English language itself. The characteristics of English present problems, but more importantly, they present enormous opportunities for the translator from a European language. Typically other languages find themselves forced into an approximation of some of the dynamics of the English language. In the same sort of process, migrants from all over the world have had a significant impact on particular aspects of European linguistic practices. To speak of a kebab, or a chicken tikka, or a curry wurst is absolutely common place in European capitals. In demotic speech, for example, one might talk about going to "un fast food" for "un type kebab". In much the same way, the penetration of English as a source, not only of vocabulary, but also of concepts and imagery, is indisputable.

'On the other side of the coin, this process can operate in reverse, because of the porous and (to a large extent) uncontrollable nature of English usage, together with the widespread existence of European roots in English grammar and vocabulary. It is now a daily occurrence for conferences, meetings, reports, debates to be held in English, wherever they may happen to be – Valencia, Riga, Frankfurt, Budapest or Brussels. Anything, in fact, in which Europeans want to signal internationalism tends to be conducted in English. The consequence is that an interesting and specific variety of English (Euro-English?) has begun to emerge throughout Europe. Its diverse branches tend, fascinatingly, to draw on specific linguistic features of specific nations. Certain English words, indeed, have entered a broad variety of languages. You may find people using a word like "exact" or "precise" to mean the same things anywhere in Europe. Bump into another person in the supermarket in Helsinki, and they are likely to say "sorry", and so on, and so on. This is a process which furnishes administrators, artists, educationalists, activists and politicians throughout Europe with an essential tool for communicating with each other, but they bring with them their native idioms and concepts which become part of the way they speak and write English. That is to say a European-English has begun to develop, which sounds and feels different to the English spoken by the English or by the Americans, or indeed by the Nigerians or the Malaysians.

'On the other hand, translating European languages has, by convention, been an issue of transposing European idioms and concepts into our familiar English words and expressions; but this is a practice which, inevitably, loses a major part of the national linguistic identity with which Europeans have been investing their own version and versions of English. Communicating the sheer richness of autochthonous speech therefore benefits enormously from an approach which takes advantage of the way that Europeans, in this case

Romanians, interject their own linguistic arrangements into the business of speaking English. As one discovers every day, in the new Europe it is perfectly possible to speak and write English, grammatically and fluently, while still sounding like a German or an Italian, and still bringing those native values into a discourse which enriches, rather than enfeebles the translation.'

Romanian Blues

Phillips extolled the virtues of two other Romanian novels to me. One was *Kill the General* (*Ucide i generalul*) by **Bogdan Hrib**. Stelian Munteanu, lover, killer and Bucharest boy, is a hero who tells us more than we ever imagined about our times. Stelian, a book editor with a sideline in international police work, has to kill a man, a general whose book he's just published. Will he pull the trigger? *Kill the General* is an exciting and suspenseful thriller. It is also a complex and detailed character study of an individual – a rollercoaster ride through the transitions which have taken place over the last few decades in Romanian history. *Kill the General* constitutes a bridge between several different phases of recent Romanian history, and outlines the differences and continuities between several different generations of Romanians over the last four decades. By his own account, Bogdan Hrib set out to construct a psychological novel which would, in part, dissect and explore how the traumas of life under a dictatorship had determined individuals' attitudes and behaviour. In fact, *Kill the General* goes a long way beyond the merely 'psychological' and turns out to be a remarkable panorama encapsulating the pressures of a rapidly changing state, and their effect on individuals.

Hrib began writing his novel in 2010, partly as a response to the current debates across Europe about the after effects of former totalitarian regimes. In the process *Kill the General* developed as an exciting and suspenseful thriller, as well as a series of reflections about the Romanian way of life (and death) over the last four decades.

It is not only the novel's suspense, characterisation and intricate plotting which holds it together, however. There is also an acute feeling for the detail of twentieth-century history, based on the life story of Hrib's hero, Stelian Munteanu, who, as the novel progresses, inhabits the roles of schoolboy, student, army recruit, and craftsman. Finally, after the Revolution introduces new freedoms he becomes an entrepreneur, travelling in various European capitals – Vienna, Copenhagen, London.

Humour is a Weapon

I asked Bo Hrib how important the political aspect in his fiction is for him. Were his books designed to entertain – or comment on society – or both? 'For a country like Romania,' he told me, 'with almost fifty years of unyielding Communist rule (from 1945, after WWII, until December 1989), the political aspect in literature, I think, is extremely important. But perhaps I should define my own concerns as social *and* political. Even between WWI and WWII, when Romania was mostly a democratic country, we had some seismic events, such as a slew of assassinations, political and otherwise (two prime ministers, other politicians, important scientists etc.) Fiction has to reflect such a tragic background for a country. In Romania, crime fiction (or "romanele poli iste") is regarded rather disdainfully, rather in the way that American "B" movies once were. It isn't important, intellectual, high-quality literature... at least not for the critics. Obviously, I don't agree. Romanian crime fiction is more social and political than even Nordic Noir. Everybody here has a family history linked with the oppression of the Communist period. And I think we're at the beginning of a new wave of Romanian novels – with the plots mixing the present and past, channelling the history of the last sixty years, perhaps as in the work of Jo Nesbo. The Romanian *Securitate* or Romanian Iron Guard from the forties can play a part, even today. During the Communist period, humour was a key weapon for writers... now, thankfully, we can write anything. So, entertaining is something my books (hopefully) do, but the Romanian crime novel is shot through with socio-political concerns.'

Anatomical Clues (*Indicii anatomice*) by **Oana Stoica-Mujea**, the other book Mike Phillips recommended, has body parts cropping up in unusual places, with an agoraphobic cop put on the case. The leading character, Iolanda Stireanu, is a brilliant detective but tormented by unsolved issues.

However, before leaving Phillips himself, I must mention one of his own books, co-written with Stejarel Olaru: the non-fiction title *Rimaru: Butcher of Bucharest*. Certain books create their effects by an inexorable accretion of detail, maintaining a firm grip on the reader's attention – and *Rimaru: Butcher of Bucharest* is most certainly in this company. The surrealistic idea of a relentless serial killer in a communist country (here, Romania) in itself exerts a certain fascination, but Mike Phillips & Stejarel Olaru, faced with a choice of approaches, have wisely opted for a cool, uninflected narrative that allows the facts to speak for themselves – to chilling effect. The circumstances surrounding the bloody career of the serial murderer Rimaru were subject to the customary secrecy *de rigueur* in a communist state, but after Romania was liberated from its communist yoke more details of the facts began to be available, and *Rimaru: Butcher of Bucharest* utilises the information uncovered by Phillips and the Romanian historian Olaru to telling effect. What comes across most clearly in this story is the customary banality of evil, but also the fashion in which that evil can flourish in a totalitarian state. It is a chilling and salutary read.

SCANDICRIME REVISITED

What this section isn't

Even without my publisher gently reminding me, I knew that there had to be a Scandinavian element to any book called *Euro Noir* (it's in the title, isn't it?) but I had a problem: how to make the Nordic section of the book you're holding different from the extensive coverage I'd applied to the field in *Nordic Noir* and *Death in a Cold Climate*? There had to be – surely! – a mention of the iconic, groundbreaking status of **Maj Sjöwall** and her partner **Per Wahlöö** (and you've just read it). And **Henning Mankell**, and **Peter Høeg**, and... well, it wouldn't be possible to namecheck everybody, would it? But what to omit to avoid too much overlap? Actually, in the event, it was relatively easy; so much has happened since I wrote those two books, and there was so much new material to hand. But I should point out that this section doesn't attempt to be a general overview of the whole Scandicrime field and its history; it's more, as other sections attempt to be for other countries, a snapshot taking us (in piecemeal fashion) into the second decade of the twenty-first century.

Watching the Swedish Detectives

Over a glass of wine (or three), conversations with Dr Steven Peacock, Reader in Film and Television Aesthetics at the University of Hertfordshire, are always lively and instructive. It's hard to say no to his suggestions (such as contributing to his book *Stieg Larsson's Millennium Trilogy*), but I was particularly interested in talking about Steven's *Swedish Crime Fiction: Novel, Film, Television*, an early proof of which he'd sent to me. His book is clearly not intended to be a buyer's guide, and its usefulness and application lies in his strip-mining of the various elements (sociopolitical, interpersonal) that illuminate the books and films Peacock has chosen for discussion.

The book takes a variety of provocative approaches to the way in which Swedish crime fiction, film and TV can offer sociopolitical insights and observations; principally through the cold-eyed observations of the (often damaged) detective protagonists. But setting is also illuminated as, for instance, in the section on the treatment of the town of Ystad (as characterised in the various series of *Wallander*) and he draws clear distinctions between the very different treatments of the area in the three series, from a variety of points of view. This section also ties in neatly to a consideration of the great commercial success of the company Yellow Bird, behind so many of the highly successful Swedish crime fiction franchises from Henning Mankell onwards.

He told me: 'I'm interested in the contrast between ideas of the perfectibility of Scandinavian society (a notion still maintained – in the teeth of evidence to the contrary – by such Nordic writers as **Gunnar Staalesen**). Notions of modernity are close to the heart of many Swedish crime narratives – and in particular the use of technology in the *Millennium* trilogy of Larsson. In another area, the very different fictional worlds of, say, **Johan Theorin** and **Mari Jungstedt**, illuminate both the more picturesque landscapes of the former (with their windswept Swedish islands out of season) and the more cosmopolitan urban areas of the latter.'

Taking Steven Peacock's ideas further, I'd point out that Swedish crime fiction sports other important themes such as examining the success (or otherwise) of microcosmic social experiments, and the irony of Sweden espousing a particular vision of socialism despite the inequalities to be found in the country's infrastructure. Nordic crime fiction in general balances the contrast between an idealised vision of a unified Scandinavian society and the sometimes eccentric personal vision of the same by the crime fiction protagonist.

Crime from the North

It is the crime fiction of the Nordic nations that is most forensically analytical. It is frustrating for many residents of Scandinavia that Sweden is often considered a sort of catch-all generic term for the various countries. The reasons are not hard to see: the massive Swedish successes in terms of exports, both cultural and commercial, and the long-held view that the country's enlightened politics represent a perfect exemplar for other nations (although that is a view challenged by the country's crime writers).

The geographical relocation of the crime genre northwards was initiated by the unprecedented success of **Peter Høeg's** *Miss Smilla's Feeling for Snow* (1992), spreading before us an intriguing new topography for the crime fiction genre. That book's stamping ground, vividly evoked, was Copenhagen and Denmark. But *Miss Smilla* was merely the tip of the iceberg: the Scandinavian territories afforded a new panoply, with the Swede **Henning Mankell** as the standard bearer, chronicling the darkly mesmerising narratives of Kurt Wallander. Other possibilities in this new literary landscape include an exploration of **Åke Edwardson's** criminous Gothenburg, or the Reykjavik of **Arnaldur Indriðason**, or **Karin Fossum's** psychologically bleak Norway. As for Sweden, the all-flattening juggernaut that was the *Millennium* trilogy of the late **Stieg Larsson** broke all sales records. Exhilarating though this Nordic crime is, it has one over-arching theme: the Scandinavian social democratic ideal is perhaps not dead, but it is fractured. The Scandinavians now inhabit the same universe as all of us.

Boyd Tonkin, the ex-literary editor of the *Independent* (now succeeded by Arifa Akbar), told me an interesting fact about Iceland. 'The writer Sjón' he remarked, 'said that the detective genre didn't really exist there before Arnaldur Indriðason got going – but he's sold 8 million worldwide so far...' Tonkin has pointed out how far Icelandic words have always travelled. 'From the thirteenth century, the epic feuds and loves of the sagas took root in the wider world's imagination,' he said.' In a ruggedly lovely island of empty spaces and harsh lives, the storyteller's words never lost their near-occult force.' Tonkin points out that Iceland is a nation that bothers to nurture its indigenous writers and that (like Norway) it even boasts a stipend system to support authors with individual works – perhaps not surprising in a society in which language is so fiercely prioritised. 'Of course,' he continues, 'Iceland also yielded to the temptations of reckless globalisation, its madly greedy banks collapsed after 2008 and brought the entire country to its knees. Then the value of culture soon reasserted itself.' But the ancient storytelling culture under discussion here has been transmuted into the crime novel, the modern day barometer of the ills of society – all of which are exacerbated by both individual venality and national disasters such as the banking crash.

The Rise of the Scandibrit

Quentin Bates ruefully notes that I coined an inelegant word for writers such as himself and **Michael Ridpath**, British novelists who write Nordic Noir: 'Scandibrits'. (I did, I should point out, coin the word in a wine bar.) But Bates (as well as being a key resource for me on all things Icelandic) is a highly talented writer and journalist who made the move into fiction with a series of crime novels set in present-day Iceland. Through a chain of coincidences, he found himself working in Iceland for his gap year. One year turned into ten, and after ten years working on the sea and a move back to the UK, Bates took to dry land and began work as a nautical journalist and editor of a commercial fishing magazine. His Gunnhildur Gisladottir series was born through the author's own inside knowledge of Iceland and its society, along with exploring the world of crime. 'There's no shortage of crime writers in Iceland these days,' he said to me. 'But it hasn't always been that way. Until a few years ago, crime was rather looked down upon. A few people dabbled, but while translated crime sold well in Iceland, especially around the hugely important Christmas market when a book is the default gift of choice, there was remarkably little homegrown stuff.

'There are exceptions. **Viktor Arnar Ingólfsson** has been writing his own brand of thriller for many years, the first of which appeared in the seventies. He once told me that, when he started, the book lists were dominated by maritime stories and memoirs, as well as foreign thrillers (Desmond Bagley was a big seller in Iceland, as he set one book there), but today it's all crime and the maritime stuff has all but vanished. Everything has changed and it's largely down to **Arnaldur Indriðason** and **Yrsa Sigurðardóttir**. Their success, and not least their success overseas, has lifted Icelandic crime writing to new levels and you can hardly move without bumping into a crime writer or a budding one somewhere. Arnaldur really kicked it all off as he brought a gritty new feel to Icelandic crime, presumably due to his having been steeped in film as a cinema critic. Yrsa came to crime after having written successfully as a children's author. Both of them seemed to be able to produce work that combined the small-town feel that Iceland has with a detachment that gave them a more international feel, while both were clearly writing with a domestic audience in mind. It's worth a mention that both had the tremendous good fortune to be translated by the late

Bernard Scudder, an absolutely outstanding translator who really was able to give Arnaldur's and Yrsa's books an added spice.

'My feeling is that the fact that they were picked up by foreign publishers gave them a new respectability, especially as relatively few Icelandic authors of any genre could get published overseas – apart from Halldór Laxness, Iceland's only Nobel Prize winner. We can say that Icelandic crime fiction was finally taken seriously, both at home and abroad, due to the efforts of Arnaldur and Yrsa,' Bates continued. 'Several Icelanders have won awards and prizes, not least Arnaldur for winning the Gold Dagger, prompting the International Dagger to be set up. Most recently he has been awarded the RBA Literary Prize in Spain for his latest novel published on 1 November 2013, with simultaneous publication in Icelandic and Spanish. British and American readers will probably have to wait a few years until *Skuggasund* appears in English. It puts him in some exalted company; previous winners are Michael Connelly, Patricia Cornwell, Philip Kerr, Andrea Camilleri and Harlan Coben.

'These days there are only five Icelandic crime writers published in English. There are Arnaldur and Yrsa, and **Viktor Arnar Ingólfsson** has belatedly appeared in English courtesy of Amazon Crossing with *The Flatey Enigma, House of Evidence* and *Daybreak*. Then there's **Árni Thórarinsson's** *Season of the Witch*, also published by Amazon, and **Stefán Máni's** *The Ship*, published by an Australian publisher and I've never seen a copy of it. That's all. It's worth mentioning that all of them had appeared in German, French and other languages before they were picked up by English language publishers. I couldn't say if this is because their work may appeal more to a German audience or if it simply reflects on the reluctance of US and UK publishers to bet on translated fiction.

'It still took Arnaldur a while to find his feet in English. His first two Erlendur books, *Synir Duftsins* (*Sons of the Dust*) and *Dauðarósir* (*Silent Kill*) were never translated, and to be brutally honest, these weren't on a par with the magnificent stuff that has been translated – I know, as I read them both when they first appeared. There are plenty more waiting to make it into English. **Ævar Örn Jósepsson** has been widely translated, as have **Agnar Jónasson, Lílja Sigurðardóttir** and the half-Icelandic, half-Czech philosophy graduate **Óttar M Norðfjörð**, who lives in Spain. And they are still coming. Debut author **Sólveig Pálsdóttir's** book *Leikarinn* (*The Actor*) was published last year to immediate acclaim, followed by *Hinir Réttlátu* (*The Righteous*), with rights sold to a German publisher. There are new faces appearing all the time, not to mention a few who are less active, such as **Jón Hallur Stefánsson** and maverick filmmaker and former MP **Thráinn Bertelsson** who has also penned a series of crime stories. Unlike Norway, with its Easter crime fiction season, most of Iceland's book business centres around the Christmas market. Arnaldur and Yrsa both have a book out every year for the Xmas market, and Arnaldur's annual offering, traditionally published on the first of November each year, has become a focal point. People discuss the 'new Arnaldur' in offices and workshops through November. Publishers have also recently tried to engineer a largely artificial competition as an advertising gimmick between the two top-selling crime writers that was essentially meaningless and which probably didn't work.

'The traditional snobbery over crime fiction not being literature appears not to have disappeared, but has at least ebbed. Icelandic publishers, like everyone else in the country, have been hit by the banks collapsing in 2008. Publishers don't have so much cash to spend, and consumers don't have nearly as much disposable income as they did before the Crash. Domestic authors are getting more attention as publishers are far less willing to invest in a translation of a foreign book unless it's a sure-fire seller: Camilla Läckberg, Jo Nesbo, Jussi Adler-Olsen, Sara Blædel and Stieg Larsson are the ones that spring to mind – all Nordic authors.

'Icelanders don't read other Nordic languages like they used to. In the past, the second language was Danish and, until a generation or two ago, Danish books were everywhere, as well as the ubiquitous Donald Duck comics that were imported from Denmark. It is said that the largest single blow to Icelanders' command of Danish was when Donald Duck was translated into Icelandic, so youngsters no longer had to struggle through the Danish versions. These days (American) English is overwhelmingly the second language, courtesy of the internet and cable TV. A great many Icelanders are entirely comfortable reading English and the publisher who used to translate Ian Rankin told me a few years ago that he had to give up. Icelanders just bought the Rebus books as they appeared in English and weren't going to wait six months for a translation to appear.

'It would be unfair not to mention **Jógvan Isaksen**, the Faroe Islands' only crime writer. He has been publishing a book every few years for a long time, with a few translated into Danish and Icelandic. Iceland and the Faroes are certainly not the same and Jógvan Isaksen's books are subtly different in feel and atmosphere with a peculiarly Faroese tone that it's very difficult to put your finger on.

'Norway and Iceland both suffer badly from small nation syndrome. Denmark and Sweden don't. Perhaps a throwback to the colonial past? Denmark and Sweden were the colonial powers, while Iceland and Norway were historically the underdogs? Or because Sweden and Denmark have historically been trading nations? There are some less salubrious sides to the various Nordic characters that don't appear until you look closely. They all look largely similar from a distance, but very different close to. I'm sure somewhere there's a PhD for someone in all this.'

The Heavy Hitters

Moving on from Quentin Bates's cogent Icelandic crime analysis, I should mention the heavy hitters from the other Nordic nations. In the early twenty-first century, the popularity of Scandinavian crime fiction (in non-Scandinavian countries) shows few signs of abating, although its death knell has been sounded on several occasions – sometimes by writers from other countries, muttering resentfully about the juggernaut which is Nordic Noir. Readers are now very familiar with the key names in the field – **Henning Mankell, Stieg Larsson, Camilla Läckberg, Jo Nesbo, Karin Fossum** – and the simultaneous steamrolling impact of Scandinavian television crime drama in which the difficult heroines of the series *The Killing* and *The Bridge* outdo each other in being barely socialised. And that's not all – there is a sizable second wave of writers (notably **Johan Theorin** with his atmospheric, slightly fey novels) whose books have received a *succès d'estime* if not breakthrough sales. (Not that their UK publishers haven't tried hard – these days, hopefully gritted teeth accompany the push for each new name.) But writers such as Theorin are, if anything, held in high regard simply because they are widely considered to be caviar to the general – novels that make more demands of the reader than more easily accessible fare, but offer richer and more complex rewards. And as this wide diversity of fascinating material from the Scandinavian countries continues to appear – and to transfix English-speaking readers – some writers who have not yet made a mark in Britain (such as the Dane **Sara Blaedel**) are enjoying second sorties into the English market after initial publication which failed to give them their due in terms of sales. But in the midst of all this diverse publishing activity and varying levels of reader attention (or its opposite), where are we to place **Dan Turèll**?

Dan Turèll: Murder in the Dark

Aficionados of the genre have long been aware that, although they may not have actually read his work, Turèll's is a name that commands respect. In the UK, he is (at present) a name for cognoscenti. And to say that situation needs remedying is something of an understatement – it's a woeful fact which one can only hope the publication of his novel *Murder in the Dark* (something of a calling card book for the author) will remedy. Not that the belated notice for this most quirkily talented Danish crime writer will bring him any pleasure this side of the grave. Like several of his chain-smoking crime-writing confrères (such as Stieg Larsson and Per Wahlöö), the author's nicotine addiction brought about an early death in 1993 (at the age of 47) from oesophageal cancer. But in his short life, Dan Turèll proved to be both prodigiously talented and versatile in his achievement with an impressive tally of novels and journalism, plus some distinguished poetry to his name.

The author is considered to be a native of Copenhagen, but was actually born in nearby Vangede, then a bucolic setting which gave him a life-long appreciation of Arcadian values. However, this was not to be the literary territory in which he moved. His best work is undeniably urban, and it is the dynamic of city life that produced his most provocative work. (His birthplace, in fact, has now been incorporated into greater Copenhagen.) Turèll has not been a prophet without honour in his own country – in the same way that the matchless private eye novels of **Gunnar Staalesen** have been honoured by a statue of his detective Varg Veum in the latter's stamping grounds of Bergen in Norway, a section of the town square of Halmtorvet in Copenhagen now enjoys the soubriquet 'Uncle Danny's Square' as a tribute to the late writer. (The renaming took place on what would have been the writer's 60th birthday.) Turèll had a taste for smoky jazz cellars, and his interest in improvised music is hardly surprising, given his involvement in the writings of the counterculture novelists and poets of the late 1940s and 1950s; similarly, his enthusiasm for Zen and mind-altering substances is of a part with this involvement. Perhaps from a modern perspective it might be observed that his rejection of the accoutrements of bourgeois culture was supplemented by a new and equally constricting set of enthusiasms, prescribed quite as stiflingly as the chintz curtains and churchgoing of the society he rejected. However, in the final analysis, Turèll was very much his own man, and the final effect of his work is diffuse in the best possible sense, not wholeheartedly subscribing to one particular set of values.

As rendered in various translations (such as the version by Mark Mussari of *Murder in the Dark*), Turèll's highly personal syntax is very much part of his appeal, with its curious digressions into arcane areas and sudden bursts of stream of consciousness. All of these stylistic tics are absolutely appropriate in this novel concerning the bloody-minded, rebellious reporter/sleuth who is the narrator ('I sighed audibly to my record player, my tape recorder, and my whiskey bottle – my three best friends – and took a cab to *The News*. I never drive myself anymore. It's my only, albeit significant, contribution to Greater Road Safety. I've saved at least three lives that way.') As Turèll's protagonist finds himself drawn into the investigation of the death of a man who phoned him with an inexplicable message, we are confronted with a character close to the shambolic anti-heroes of the great English thriller writer Eric Ambler whose non-professional heroes tend to stumble upon the truth rather than follow a coherent through-line. This English echo is surprising, given that Turèll's literary models (in terms of his crime fiction work at least) would, one might have thought, have been American. The author was fascinated by that country and its writers, even though his sympathy always remained with the American underdog and outsiders such as the beat poets and writers. In his writings, he cast a notably cool eye upon the more conventional pieties of American society. His choice of a reporter as protagonist is inevitably granted verisimilitude by his own journalistic skills. Turèll was as prolific in this field as in anything else he wrote, and his range of subjects (from literature to comic strips to politics) demonstrated a truly omnivorous level of interest in culture, both high and low. His celebrated 'Murder Series' is in the Chandler/Hammett genre, and the books are designed to be discrete, separate entries, so that they may be read out of sequence. This particular circumstance will mean that as (hopefully) more Turèll novels become available in English, readers will have no cause for complaint. There will be no repetition of the kind of displeasure readers felt in trying to cope with the oeuvre of such writers as Håkan Nesser and Jo Nesbo, which appeared in the UK out of chronological sequence.

Murder in the Dark sports a winning combination of engaging crime narrative and a cool, unsentimental appraisal of Scandinavian society as seen through the eyes of its shabby, unconventional anti-hero. It provides a good impression of the writer's idiosyncratic approach to popular form. While the shibboleth-breaking nature of his poetry perhaps represents his most unorthodox work, even this book, written within the parameters of the detective genre, bears many of his fingerprints: it is slightly off-kilter, vaguely experimental. Though the novel is apparently linear in its progression, Turèll is perfectly prepared to break with the standard narrative form for quixotic asides before taking us back to the imperatives of the crime novel. His eccentric protagonist has many echoes of the author himself, who enjoyed shocking his audience, not least through his own odd dress sense, and his taste for having his fingernails painted with black polish. 'Épater la bourgeoisie!' were his watchwords, and the nature of his rebellion was inspired by such beat writers as Jack Kerouac and William Burroughs. In terms of his poetry, Allen Ginsberg was a key influence, but in his novels (the autobiographical *Images of Vangede* and even the detective novels) he perhaps shows the influence of the American writer Nelson Algren, with an iconoclastic hero who is just about able to function within the constricting terms of polite society.

There are elements of *Murder in the Dark* which now seem quite as relevant as when they were written, such as the cover-ups which were par for the course for well-connected paedophiles in the media. ('The entire country had admired him… it was only a minority… who knew he had been a paedophile, and that minority wisely kept its mouth shut. You don't want to shut down your own workplace.') But like all the most accomplished writing in the Nordic Noir field, there is an acute and well-observed sense of place throughout the book – and the descriptions of Copenhagen (via the on-the-ropes narrator) channel the poetic sensibility which is the author's own: 'Copenhagen is at its most beautiful when seen out of a taxi at midnight, right at that magical moment when one day dies and another is born, and the printing presses are buzzing with the morning newspapers…'

Up-to-date with Håkan Nesser

The Strangler's Honeymoon (which appeared in the UK in 2013) was notably darker in tone than most entries for Håkan Nesser's ageing ex-copper Van Veeteren. Desperately lonely, sixteen-year-old Monica Kammerle has little idea of what she is getting herself into when she begins an affair with her mother's latest partner, the sophisticated Benjamin Kerran. Months later, when a woman's strangled body is found decomposing in her flat, the Maardam police must discover who has committed this terrible crime. It isn't long before they realise the perpetrator may have killed before – and is likely to do so again. Meanwhile former Chief Inspector Van Veeteren finds himself drawn into the mystery when a priest, who has learned dreadful secrets, appeals to him for help. But when the priest falls beneath the wheels of a train and the police find more dead ends than leads, it seems Van Veeteren will have to come up with a new approach to unearth this dark serial killer, before he chooses his next victim. Håkan Nesser is one of Sweden's most popular crime writers, receiving numerous awards for his novels featuring Inspector Van Veeteren, including the European Crime Fiction Star Award (Ripper Award) 2010/11, the Swedish Crime Writers' Academy Prize (three times) and Scandinavia's Glass Key Award. The Van Veeteren series is published in over 25 countries and has sold over 10 million copies worldwide.

Gaute Heivoll: Before I Burn

A variety of questions may be asked about Gaute Heivoll's novel *Before I Burn*, which arrived on UK shores weighed down with encomiums. Is it a literary or a crime novel? And if the latter, might it be considered part of the current all-conquering Scandinavian crime wave? One of those singing its praise is the writer Karin Fossum, and Heivoll's publisher is canny to emblazon the jacket with her quote ('One of the best books I have ever read') as she is acclaimed as the finest wielder of language in the Nordic noir field. Is *Before I Burn* more of the same? Certainly, this luminously written novel qualifies as 'literature' – particularly in Don Bartlett's sympathetic translation – but for all its playing with shifting timeframes and self-reflexivity (Heivoll makes himself part of the narrative), the book still has at its centre a dangerous criminal.

In the 1970s, a cloistered community in rural Norway experiences a daily terror as a pyromaniac appears set on destroying the town. Civic panic is the order of the day – as is a large dose of paranoia. Neighbour regards neighbour suspiciously, wondering who is behind the arson, while one woman in particular finds her life torn apart, as she slowly realises that the firestarter is her son.

The Norwegian author has under his belt some charming children's books and poetry, none of which prepares the reader for the deeply unsettling experience on offer here. Heivoll is particularly adroit at conveying the growing unease of a community under siege, and his evocation of the conflagrations is shot through with a kind of poetic imagery that removes the book from the parameters of crime fiction ('The smoke was rising through the cracks in the floor, collecting and advancing to the ceiling. In front of her eyes a serene figure of smoke appeared to be slowly taking shape. It had arms, hands, feet and a hazy face…'). More problematic is the risky strategy that Heivoll adopts of running his own childhood in parallel with the narrative. The author clearly feels a kind of psychic link to the arsonist, and finds his own youth transformed by the town's trauma, with the inevitable separation of parent from child a central metaphor in the book. Although elegantly written, *Before I Burn* is a book full of pain: the destruction of lives, the narrator's father dying of cancer, and an unsparing examination of the darker recesses of the human psyche. But if Heivoll draws back from explaining the mental processes of his murderous doppelgänger, any frustration on the part of the reader (in that we are granted no closure), is a small price to pay. Treating the final mystery of a human evil as an unknowable thing gives the book a resonance that lives beyond its pages. Those seeking the more immediate pleasures of a crime narrative should look elsewhere, but Heivoll's unhurried prose satisfyingly addresses the mysteries of memory and the precariousness of human existence.

Liza Marklund and The Hammers

If the sources of modern Scandinavian crime fiction are to your taste, the formidable Swede **Liza Marklund** remains a lodestone. She shares the sobriquet of 'The Godmother' of the genre with Maj Sjöwall (who long outlived her fellow crime fiction progenitor Per Wahlöö), though Marklund is much younger. The latter's taut *Lifetime* (2013) is typically unadorned and compelling fare, beginning with the most famous police officer in Sweden found murdered in his bed, and his son missing. It's a characteristically lean and focussed example of Marklund's series featuring investigative reporter Annika Bengtzon.

By contrast, more recent entrants in the genre are the Hammers, Danes **Lotte and Søren Hammer**, whose *The Hanging* (2013, first in a six-part series) is a truly unusual novel from the brother and sister team who are already enjoying much acclaim in their native country. I asked all three writers how long they felt the current UK fascination with their genre would continue. 'For some time yet,' Liza Marklund said to me.

'I'd like a lot more people in the UK to be reading me... and adopting Annika Bengtzon as a role model with her "take no shit from anyone philosophy!". The Hammers were more tentative. 'I really have no idea' replied the quietly spoken Lotte (a very different personality from her more ebullient brother). 'We have yet to make the impact outside of Denmark and the German territories that we'd like to... so we are fervently hoping the UK obsession with Scandicrime has some life yet. At least until we're – hopefully – taken up.'

Michael Katz Krefeld: The Raven Sequence

Derailed by Michael Katz Krefeld is the first in a new sequence about Inspector Thomas Ravnsholdt , known to his friends and colleagues as 'Ravn', with no 'e'. The books are being marketed as the 'Ravn' series in Scandinavia. This novel arrives with the best of pedigrees: it's handled by the all-powerful Salomonsson agency in Sweden, holders of the international rights for some of the most heavyweight names in Nordic Noir. And *Derailed*, after appearing in Denmark, quickly assumed second place in the bestseller lists, and has been lucky enough to enjoy a sympathetic translation by Paul Russell Garrett, who does full justice to the text. (One might expect no less from such a knowledgeable aficionado of the genre, as I know from frequent meetings with him at various events.)

Krefeld made his debut as a crime writer in 2007 with *Before the Storm*, featuring as protagonist a doctor, Maja Holm. Her investigation of a dangerous conspiracy (in which she is co-opted by a television journalist) marked the writer out as an individual talent, but *Derailed* bids fair to be the author's breakthrough book. Thomas Ravnsholdt is on sick leave from the city police after the savage killing of his girlfriend during a home robbery. Suffering agonies of guilt, Ravn has retired to the boat he owns in Christianshavn canal, his only companion his dog. Then a friend enlists his aid in tracking down a young girl who vanished some years earlier, and before long Ravn is back on his old turf and investigating the Copenhagen underworld. Is the missing girl a victim of human trafficking, sold to the unpleasant Slavros, owner of a string of brothels in Europe? In Garrett's intelligent translation, the Danish writer is something different in the all-conquering wave of Scandinavian crime fiction writers. His work is fast-moving and cinematic (as befits his work on a variety of television series), sporting a powerful sense of locale and a highly individual detective in the troubled but tenacious Ravn. This looks set to be one of the most promising crime series around.

Lars Kepler: Two Who Are One

Lars Kepler is a bifurcated writer. After the great success of *The Hypnotist*, intrigued Swedes (in what became something of a news story) learned that the name was a pseudonym, subsequently stripped away to reveal a husband and wife team – both low-profile literary authors – writing together. 'Lars Kepler' is the nom-de-plume of Alexandra and Alexander Ahndoril. After the compelling *The Hypnotist* – a book that gleaned bestseller status in Sweden – their follow-up novels were keenly awaited. The duo told me on a trip to London that they see themselves as part of a Swedish crime novel tradition. 'We enjoy taking our part in the tradition,' they said, 'but we are also rebelling against it when we're attempting to incorporate something innovative. The team's subsequent novels, the very differentiated *The Fire Witness*, *The Sandman* and *The Nightmare*, demonstrate their reluctance to traverse over-familiar paths. *The Fire Witness* (2013) in particular is characteristically scabrous, with DI Joona Linn investigating a home for troubled girls

Conquering Germany: Jussi Adler-Olsen

Walk into any major bookshop in Germany, and you will see that the crime section is often dominated by the work of a man born not in Deutschland but in Denmark. His books customarily storm the German fiction charts and three of them held the top three spots on *Der Spiegel*'s fiction chart for 60 consecutive weeks. To say that Jussi Adler-Olsen is at the very top of the crime fiction tree doesn't do him justice, and his novels featuring the bloody-minded, sometimes under-motivated detective Carl Mørck – repeatedly proving, with the aid of his counterintuitive Muslim assistant Assad, that he is smarter than his dismissive superiors – are unsparing, sometimes gruesome and always utterly compelling. These are not books for the squeamish, but for those who like strong meat in their fiction, and such titles as *Mercy* (2011, translated by Lisa Hartford) and *Disgrace* (2012, Penguin, translated by Lisa Hartford), are required reading for the aficionado.

What is particularly impressive about Adler-Olsen's sleuth is the fact that as well as being damaged (what contemporary detective isn't these days?), Carl Mørck is also somewhat lazy. Close reading of one of the writer's labyrinthine narratives makes it clear that there is an unusual strategy at work: the roles of Holmes and Watson in Mørck and his assistant Assad are actually reversed, although this may not be immediately apparent. The real imaginative leaps are made by the unworldly, maladroit Assad, who is shaping up to be one of the great creations of modern crime fiction.

Sara Blaedel: The Danish Crime Queen

Massively successful in the German and Scandinavian countries, Danish Crime Queen Sarah Blaedel had clearly not made the impact in the UK that was her due. 2013 saw an energetic re-launch, with a new translation (by Erik J. Macki and Tara F. Chace) of *Blue Blood*, repositioning (the publishers no doubt hope) her detective Louise Rick in the correct place she deserves in British readers' estimation. In an idyllic neighbourhood of Copenhagen, a young woman, Susanne Hansson, is discovered in her apartment bound and gagged, the victim of an extraordinarily brutal rape attack. Detective Inspector Louise Rick soon learns that Susanne met the rapist on a popular online dating site, although Susanne tries to conceal this. Events quickly spiral out of control as a horrified Louise realises that the rapist is using the website to target specific women for future attacks. It's not long before the next assault leads to a death and Louise finds herself in the middle of a full-blown murder investigation. Undercover and in danger in a world of faceless dating, Louise must try and stop a murderer who has shocked Copenhagen to its core. But how much is she willing to risk in order to catch a killer? Sara Blaedel's highly assured Louise Rick crime series has been published to great acclaim in fourteen territories around the world and each of her novels quickly attains number one position in the Danish bestseller charts. Her place in the British crime sales hierarchy may have been delayed, but the clock is ticking...

Arnaldur Indriðason: Strange Shores

When you have been christened as the King of Icelandic Crime Fiction (Yrsa Sigurðardóttir, as mentioned above, is the Queen), a certain resting on the laurels might be considered permissible. But Arnaldur Indriðason is far too rigorous a writer for that, as the valedictory *Strange Shores* (translated in customarily impeccable fashion by Victoria Cribb and published in the UK in 2013) reminds us. As with Henning Mankell's *The Troubled Man*, this is the last outing for the writer's celebrated detective – in Indriðason's case, the doughty Detective Erlendur. A young woman walks into Iceland's frozen fjords and is never seen again. But she leaves a disturbing legacy involving betrayal and revenge. Several decades later, in the same region, Erlendur is hunting for both the missing woman and a long-lost brother – the latter's disappearance during a storm when they were children has left him with a bitter lifelong legacy. He is to find, as so often before, the most sobering of answers to his questions. As ever, Indriðason's writing is a striking combination of brilliantly realised sense of place and an astringent investigation of the human psyche.

Gunnar Staalesen: Cold Hearts

The composer Mahler, forever struggling to get his work recognised, famously prophesied: 'My time will come.' And, as the Scandinavian crime wave continues to steamroller all before it, one of its most talented practitioners might be forgiven for ruefully echoing Mahler's words – at least in the UK, where he is shamefully under-regarded. Throughout the rest of Europe, Staalesen is held in the highest esteem. Those who know about such matters are well aware that he is every inch the equal of his Nordic confrères Henning Mankell and Jo Nesbo and the latter's judgement ('A Norwegian Chandler') adorns the jacket of this novel. However, his sales, in Britain at least, have remained stubbornly incommensurate with his stellar reputation, and it must rankle for this modern master of the private eye novel to see less talented writers outsell him. But perhaps *Cold Hearts* (superbly translated by Don Bartlett) will finally elevate Staalesen to the sales pantheon on which he belongs. Bergen private detective Varg Veum receives a visit from a young prostitute; her friend, Margrethe, has vanished after a terrifying encounter with one of her clients. As the relentlessly tenacious Varg tries to track down the missing girl, the body count escalates (par for the course where he is concerned) and he is to discover corruption at every level of Norwegian society, from its violent subcultures to its moneyed upper middle class.

It was by design that Staalesen chose social work as the earlier career for his sleuth; the notion of damaged psyches resulting from family trauma is a key theme. Of the quartet of Veum books that have appeared in the UK since *At Night All Wolves are Grey* in 1986, two – *Yours until Death* (1993) and *The Writing on the Wall* (2004) – have featured such issues. Staalesen once told me that he felt Scandinavian crime fiction in general – and notably that from Sweden and Norway – has a salutary characteristic: a concentration on sociopolitical issues woven into the narrative schema, often with a critical anatomising of the less appealing side of Scandinavia's welfare societies – as in *Cold Hearts*. Staalesen's books are among the most distinctive in the crime field, and if you have yet to discover Bergen's most bloody-minded private eye, Varg Veum, *Cold Hearts* is the perfect place to start.

Camilla Grebe & Åsa Träff: More Bitter than Death

While many writers have enjoyed great exposure during the phenomenal, continuing success of the Scandinavian crime wave, there are some names which have yet to achieve the kind of prominence which is their due. Such is the case with Camilla Grebe & Åsa Träff, who have demonstrated to those non-Nordic readers lucky enough to have encountered them that they are among the most ambitious and fastidious of novelists in the field. Grebe is a graduate of the Stockholm School of Economics, while Träff is a psychologist specialising in cognitive behavioural therapy. Between them, these two very different women have created a writing identity which is subtly unlike that of most of their contemporaries, as *More Bitter than Death* (translated by Tara Chace and published in Britain in 2014) comprehensively proves. In a Stockholm apartment, a five-year-old girl watches from underneath the kitchen table as her mother is savagely kicked to death. At the same time, in another part of town, psychotherapist Siri Bergman and her colleague Aina are dealing with new patients: a group of women who are all victims of domestic violence. There is Kattis, abused by her brutal boyfriend and living in fear of his return, and Malina, a promising young athlete who has been attacked by a man she met online. Their collective history is both scarifying and disturbing, and (like so much Nordic crime fiction) presents the male sex in a distinctly less-than-favourable light. But as the group of women begins to bond, it isn't long before the threats that reside in several of their lives infiltrate their way into their new-found peace. And the fate of the young girl who watched her mother murdered becomes intertwined with the women's group. The novel, which has been concentrating on subtle character building, is transmogrified into the narrative of the tense pursuit of a murderer. If the ethos of the book seems to belong to an earlier era (Jane Campion's recent drama *Top of the Lake* treated a similar group of abused women in much more ambiguous fashion), that is not to deny that domestic violence is a pressing issue for many women, and it is a passionate concern of the two authors here. It is that issue as much as the efficient mechanics of the thriller form which gives the novel its acidic and compelling edge.

Karin Fossum: I Can See in the Dark

There are few commentators these days who would demur from the opinion that Karin Fossum is one of the top four or five practitioners of the Scandinavian crime novel, with a grasp of psychology and the more stygian aspects of malign human behaviour that is second to none. (She is only outdone, perhaps, by the writer Ruth Rendell, with whom she is often compared – and who is a particular favourite of Scandinavian novelists, as I have discovered when interviewing some of them for various books.) The keen social critique of Fossum's novels is perhaps a more important integument of her work than it is for many of her confreres, and the latter element is well to the fore in her 2011 novel (appearing a few years later in the UK in a nuanced translation by James Anderson), *I Can See in the Dark*. This is one of the writer's most unforgiving books in terms of its examination of what used to be unequivocally called evil, but it is shot through with a humanity that finally makes it a nourishing rather than a bleak read and, inevitably, suspense is a key component of the narrative. Fossum's protagonist Riktor is angered by the way a policeman enters the house without knocking. The two have no exchanges as to why the detective is there, as Riktor thinks he knows the reason – he is, in fact, guilty of a grotesque crime. But all is not as it seems. The policeman is not seeking a missing person; he is there to accuse Riktor of something very different – ironically a crime the latter did not commit. This is Fossum on rare form, and the book is perhaps a good entry point for those who have not tried her earlier work.

Anne Holt: Death of the Demon

To readers keen to investigate new avenues of Nordic noir, it sometimes comes as a surprise to discover just how popular and prolific certain authors have been in other territories before they made their way into translation. Anne Holt is a case in point. She is one of Norway's bestselling female crime writers, who has not only worked for the Oslo Police Department and founded her own law firm, but has served as Norway's Minister of Justice – a woman to be reckoned with. The reasons why she is published in 30 languages and has sold over 6 million copies of her books may be found within the pages of *Death of the Demon*, a typically astringent and unrelenting novel set in an orphanage outside Oslo where a 12-year-old boy is wreaking havoc. The institution's director, Agnes Vestavik, is disturbed by what she sees in the boy's eyes: a burning, virulent hatred. And when Agnes is discovered at her desk stabbed in the neck with a kitchen knife – with the boy nowhere to be found – the new superintendent of police, the intuitive Hanne Wilhelmsen (familiar to Holt's admirers from other novels), is handed what looks like an open and shut case. Needless to say, it isn't.

Steffen Jacobsen: Danish/Italian Collisions

And still they come: the river of compelling crime fiction novels by Nordic authors shows not the slightest sign of running dry, as the impressive *When the Dead Awaken* proves. But the bestselling Danish author of *Trophy*, Steffen Jacobsen, is not in fact inspired by Mankell and co, but by Roberto Saviano's non-fiction epic *Gomorrah*, and the subject here is the same: the ruthless criminal organisation, the Camorra, which effectively runs Naples. More insidious and more violent than the Sicilian Mafia, its grip is total, and when a shipping container goes aground on the quay in Napoli, dozens of corpses fall out. Public Prosecutor Sabrina D'Avalos, ambitious and motivated, is given the assignment and finds links to the Camorra – and, distressingly, to her own father. Soon the Mafia's most implacable killers are on her trail. This is splendidly edgy stuff with a narrative grip that simply will not let go. Despite its plot and locale, this is a Danish rather than an Italian thriller, and Steffen Jacobsen is an impressive addition to the swelling ranks of Scandinavian crime novelists. *When the Dead Awaken* is a tense, no-nonsense thriller.

Anders de la Motte: Playing Games

Anders de le Motte's *Game Trilogy* is an international phenomenon, published to healthy sales in 27 countries and selling more than 200,000 copies in its native Sweden alone. In the first book in the sequence, *Game*, dropout Henrik 'HP' Pettersson finds a state-of-the-art mobile phone on the train and considers selling it. But then he starts receiving messages asking him to take part in challenges for reward and glory, and he quickly becomes hooked on the thrill of The Game. Each task is secretly filmed and uploaded for other 'Players' to comment on, the more daring the mission, the greater the thrill and reward for HP. The succeeding volumes, *Buzz* and *Bubble*, keep up the helter-skelter trajectory. Anders de la Motte was formerly a police officer and then director of security at one of the world's largest IT companies, and is currently freelancing as an international security consultant. *Game* received the First Book Award from the Swedish Crime Writers' Academy.

Camilla Läckberg: The Lost Boy

Her international bestseller status assured, the Swedish crime writer Camilla Läckberg continues to take a highly individual approach to the psychological crime novel, with a Christie-like attention to small town details. The setting for *The Lost Boy* is, as in most of her fiction, the author's native Fjällbacka. Detective Patrik Hedström has encountered tragedy in his own life, and a murder case focussing on Fjällbacka's deceased financial director, Mats Sverin, is a not unwelcome distraction from his own family misfortunes. Sverin was a man who people appeared to like without really knowing him. Was he a man with something to hide? His teenage inamorata, Nathalie, has just returned to the area with her young son. Is she able to illuminate the life of the enigmatic Mats? Läckberg's cool and focussed narrative is notable for its careful balance.

Hans Koppel: Unwelcome Suitors

The novelist Ann Cleeves may be a keen aficionado of Nordic noir, but she recently expressed qualms over the endemic levels of sexual violence in the genre. Had she just read **Hans Koppel**? His last book, *She's Never Coming Back*, made the most excoriating work in the genre look as cosy as an episode of *Call the Midwife*. Perhaps the most unsettling thing about the book was the ritual sexual debasement and torture visited upon the luckless heroine, kept captive in a house where she could still see her distraught, unknowing family, and moving towards (spoiler alert) quite the most dispiriting, downbeat ending. It was, nevertheless, a highly professional piece of work, but alienated several critics with its overwhelming sense of hopelessness. Those readers may be reluctant to pick up Koppel's new book, *You're Mine Now*, but are they doing themselves a disservice? After all, thrillers are meant to unsettle, and Koppel is undoubtedly a master of setting the nerves on edge.

Magnus and Anna enjoy a companionable marriage, but then Anna unwisely has an affair with a colleague, Eric, she encounters at a conference, with disastrous consequences. Eric is attentive and flattering, but then Anna discovers that he has been filming her in the shower and decides to end the affair. She finds – inevitably – that she has opened the gates to something very sinister indeed. Eric's attentions become ever more threatening and Anna begins to fear for her life. Should she tell her husband or not? Or should she find a decisive way to handle Eric while keeping her secrets?

As with the last book, Koppel is highly adroit at focusing on his principal narrative engine. Once again we have a woman under threat – not, this time, a captive, but just as much the victim of a truly dangerous man (Eric has strangled his own mother). And as before, there is an internationalism of setting here that rarely dispenses any local colour – the narrative could take place in any major city. Koppel is interested in screwing the tension ever tighter, and in sinewy prose (as translated by Kari Dickson), he orchestrates that tension with authority. Those who disliked the negativity of the last book will be relieved to hear that the heroine here is better able to fight back against an appalling male predator. What is perhaps most interesting about Koppel is the truly dyspeptic view he has of his own sex – a collaboration between Andrea Dworkin and Marilyn French could not produce more cutting invective against the male gender.

New (ish) Blood: A Miscellany

In November 2013, the Swedish Crime Academy voted **Christoffer Carlsson's** *The Invisible Man from Salem* 'Best Crime Novel of the Year' in the Swedish category. Carlsson was competing with a prestigious quartet: Arne Dahl, Håkan Nesser, Johan Theorin and another writer yet to break on UK shores, **Katarina Wennstam**. The novel is the inaugural book in a planned series featuring a detective called Leo Junker. The second novel is due for publication in 2014 with Carlsson's Swedish publishers, Piratförlaget. The Swedish Crime Academy praised the author's work for being 'a strong noir novel dense with a mood of grief and hopelessness'. Previous winners include Leif G W Persson, Roslund/Hellström, Stieg Larsson, Inger Frimansson and the first-rate Swedish writer **Åsa Larsson**, among others. Born in 1986, Christoffer Carlsson obtained a Doctors degree in Criminology at the University of Stockholm, where he has lived and taught since 2005. His debut novel, the 'underground noir' *The Case of Vincent Franke*, was published to great acclaim in 2010 and became an instant bestseller in Sweden and Italy. It was also sold to several foreign publishers. His second novel, *The One-Eyed Rabbit* (2011), confirmed him as one of the most talented young names in Swedish writing, noted for its grasp of criminal psychology, his professional field.

The Gingerbread House by **Carin Gerhardsen** (2012) is, like all her books, fast-paced and addictive: she writes finely tuned pieces that demand to be read in one sitting. **Jørn Lier Horst's** *Closed for Winter* (2013) deservedly won a Booksellers' Prize. It's set on the coast of Norway in autumn, when the mists come swirling in from the sea and bloody murder is done. Markedly relentless is *Linda, as in the Linda Murder* by **Leif G W Persson** (2012), while *Where Evil Lies* by the Norwegian **Jørgen Brekke** (2013) combines the medieval fascination with anatomy and a modern-day obsession with rare books, sparking a series of brutal murders in Norway and the US. **Sander Jakobsen's** *The Preacher* (2012) explores love and guilt in Scandinavian small-town society (the name is a pseudonym for two writers).

The Other Larsson

If you're a Swedish crime writer, is it an advantage or a disadvantage to share the name of its most commercially successful practitioner? Particularly if the latter is no longer with us and there may be a gap in the market? The question must have occurred to **Åsa Larsson**, who – coincidentally? – even shares the same publisher as her late namesake (but no relation) Stieg. The jacket of her 2014 book, *The Second Deadly Sin*, is emblazoned with a quote of mine from the *Independent* comparing her with Lisbeth Salander's online begetter. In fact, though, the comparison is a touch academic. Firstly, the distaff Larsson is a very different kind of novelist, with a more literary approach to the genre and (dare one say it?) she is the better writer. This fifth novel once again features Larsson's duo of female protagonists, Inspector Anna-Maria Mella and ace prosecutor Rebecca Martinsson. We are taken to the Arctic north of Sweden where mysteries are hidden under the ice – and, as in such earlier books as *The Savage Altar*, we are not to be put in touch with the divine: religion harbours sinister and minatory secrets.

As with her earlier book *The Black Path*, Larsson has us by the throat from her first paragraph. In the tundra, a bear has been on the rampage, and the contents of its stomach disclose a gruesome revelation. And in Kurravaara, a woman has been savagely murdered, while her young grandson has also disappeared. Rebecca Martinsson's participation in the investigation is sidelined by the machinations of a rival, but she is not so easily put off; as before, though, her pursuit of an implacable murderer will put her in danger and expose a crime that stretches back over the ages. The plotting here is hardly innovative, but all of this is worked out with customary panache in Larsson's storytelling, and the set pieces are electric.

If there is nothing here to quite match the astonishing opening of *The Black Path* (in which the frozen corpse of a woman is discovered in a fisherman's ice hut), there is nevertheless that acute sense of landscape that the author evokes with great specificity. (She is less interested in urban settings than most of her confrères.) Ironic, perceptive touches quicken the narrative throughout, and the characterisation of the bloody-minded Rebecka (who Larsson really puts through the mill here) keeps *The Second Deadly Sin* firmly grounded. This is no superwoman, but a persistent individual who gets the job done. Larsson Mark II remains one of the brightest stars in the current Nordic firmament.

Jo Nesbo: Still the King

Jo Nesbo gently but firmly clutched my arm. I was to talk to him at the Manchester Literature Festival, and our names had been announced. We were heading for the stage. But just before we walked on, the creator of such phenomenally popular crime novels as *The Snowman* smiled at me and said 'Why don't you give me the big rock star build-up?' He dropped back. There is no arguing with Mr Nesbo, so I did just that: reminding a beaming audience how Nesbo's Harry Hole novels were selling one book every 23 seconds. My peroration ended with: 'And here's the reigning king of Scandinavian crime fiction: Mr Jo Nesbo!' The hall erupted as if I'd just announced Justin Bieber to an audience of tweens.

But though I'd been bumped into this salesmanship by the writer himself, Nesbo has a modest persona – despite the fact that he has every reason to assume rock star hauteur (his own albums as a singer routinely topped Norwegian charts). These days, it is, of course, his writing that has conquered the public imagination, from the gritty social commitment of *The Redbreast* (with its unsparing vision of his country's wartime past) to the blockbuster excitement of *The Snowman* and the recent *Police*. Nesbo forged something new from the cliché of the dyspeptic alcoholic copper, making Harry Hole the most successful Nordic crime export since Henning Mankell's Kurt Wallander.

Cockroaches is, in fact, the second outing for the detective, making a belated appearance in translation in this country (courtesy of Don Bartlett) after the recent – similarly late – UK debut of the writer's first novel, *The Bat*. So how does *Cockroaches*, written in 1998, read now?

Harry Hole arrives in Bangkok after the Norwegian ambassador (a close friend of the Prime Minister) is murdered in a downmarket motel, but it seems that the dead man's family has secrets they wish to keep. Harry (whose job is to fend off scandal during the investigation) lays his hands on some incendiary CCTV footage. Needless to say, a can of worms soon splits open, and when another diplomat is knifed in an Asian brothel, Harry realises that keeping a lid on things will be a tough job. *The Bat* channelled culture shock tactics with its fish-out-of-water Norwegian sleuth in Australia, and *Cockroaches* employs similar tactics with a far more rigorous attention to plotting than in the earlier book. The complex narrative and large dramatis personae are handled with steely authority, but what really makes the novel work is the fact that the picturesque seediness of Bangkok and Thailand turn out to be Harry Hole's natural element, as Nesbo plumps his hero down in a very non-Norwegian setting.

Viveca Sten: Still Waters

In 2008, Viveca Sten's debut crime novel *Still Waters* (*I de lugnaste vatten*) became an overnight success and launched her decisively on to the Swedish crime writing scene. Her 'Sandhamn Murder' series has reached seven books, with most of them bagging the number one sales slot. There has been a corresponding success in such countries as Germany and France, where readers have been intrigued by the picturesque milieu of Sandhamn and the gruesome murders endemic to the island. But the success of the series is not just limited to the printed page. Over 1.7 million Swedish viewers watched the first season of a TV miniseries based on Sten's novels when it aired in December 2010. Two more seasons followed, and the series was nominated for an award at the Kristallen Awards, the Swedish equivalent of the Emmys. Sten is a spiritual heir of Agatha Christie, and has captured the essence of the UK crime queen in her beguiling work.

The Scandinavian Crime Screen: Selected Films and TV (by date)

Van Veeteren (TV, 2000–2006, various directors)
The author likes the series! Crime writers cannot always be guaranteed to approve of TV adaptations of their books – often the reverse, in fact – but the author Håkan Nesser has expressed his approval (with reservations) of this solid, low-key series based on his estimable Van Veeteren books. Following the acceptance of Mankell's Kurt Wallander, viewers have been slower to accept a less familiar Scandinavian detective, proving perhaps that Nordic Noir admirers need to spread their net wider. Crime maestro Nesser's Van Veeteren is a veteran detective in his sixth decade, dealing uneasily with retirement (he has become an antiquarian bookseller), but unable to put aside his impeccable sleuthing instincts. Nesser's plots have justice done to them, and like the books, characterisation is to the fore. A particular

asset of the films is the playing of the urbane Sven Wollter as the ageing detective – full of psychological nuance.

Easy Money (Film, 2010, Daniel Espinosa, director)
According to the urbane crime writer-cum-lawyer Jens Lapidus, Stockholm is quite as violent and dangerous as any drug-ridden American city. *Easy Money*, the multi-stranded first book in his crime trilogy, was something different from (and on a larger canvas than) most Nordic Noir fare, and here receives a persuasive film adaptation. JW is an economics student who conceals an impoverished background by living the high life funded by contacts within the criminal world but, when he becomes involved in a murky money-laundering operation with violent Eastern European criminals, it has disastrous results – and not just for him. This is sophisticated and intelligent storytelling, dealing in a provocative fashion with the dividing line between commerce and crime, with echoes of the US TV series *Breaking Bad* as its ill-equipped protagonist is drawn into a lethal morass.

Anno 1790 (TV, 2011, Rickard Petrolius, director)
The Scandinavian crime invasion has thrown up much interesting material, and *Anno 1790* is a persuasive example of why the genre has such staying power: this compelling drama rings several very satisfying changes on established formulae. This Swedish historical crime piece (which stars Peter Eggers, Joel Spira and Linda Zilliacus) boasts an acute sense of period. Johan has served as a doctor in the Russo-Swedish war of the eighteenth century, but is now a police inspector in Stockholm. He is a modern man of the day: he rejects religion, inspired by the French revolution and Voltaire. An ill-advised love affair with the wife of his commanding officer complicates his life, as do his attempts to ensure that the revolution he desires is a bloodless one. But violent death is to remain an immovable presence in his life. The real achievement of *Anno 1790* is its canny combination of vividly realised historical detail and the suggestion of a twentieth-century consciousness in its hero. Peter Eggers is a charismatic actor who commands our attention throughout Rickard Petrolius's powerfully realised drama.

False Trail (Film, 2011, Kjell Sundvall, director)
The slow-burning but gripping *False Trail* is a sequel – definitely on the belated side – to the successful Scandinavian film by the same director

The Hunters. It was originally known (unimaginatively) as *The Hunters 2*. Its principal attraction (apart from its sinewy performances) is the exquisite photography of its sylvan locales, but the ever-reliable Rolf Lassgård, a terrifying Peter Stormare and Annika Nordin do excellent service in the acting stakes.

The Bridge Series 2 (TV, 2012, various directors)
The fascination for Scandinavian crime series inaugurated with *The Killing* continued with the quirky, mesmerising *The Bridge* – and Series II maintained (with some caveats) the iron grip of its predecessor. Björn Stein's crime drama acquired a dedicated following, eager for the second season after its serial killer nemesis was brought to justice. This time, with a more diverse group of terrorists behind various deaths, we are once again in the company of the fascinating sociopathic heroine, Saga Norén who is, if possible, even further off the spectrum of ordinary human behaviour than before, often to hilarious effect. And again, we have the female/male cop duo work together on the case (one Swedish, one Danish), marvellously played by Sofia Helin and Kim Bodnia, the latter struggling to come to terms with the trauma of what happened to him in the first series. But perfect though the amiable Bodnia was, it was (and is) the striking Sofia Helin's performance as the eccentric Saga that has made her a cult figure, particularly for those of us missing *The Killing*'s Sarah Lund.

The Hour of the Lynx (Film, 2013, Søren Kragh-Jacobsen, director)
After an impressive contribution to the Danish political drama *Borgen*, the director (and winner of a Danish Academy Award) Søren Kragh-Jacobsen has forged an intense and subtle film that showcases a performance of psychological insight by two actors best known for *The Killing*, Sofie Gråbøl and Søren Malling. Helen, a priest, is called to a secure hospital by a psychiatrist (Signe Egholm Olsen, also familiar from *Borgen*). A young man who murdered an ageing couple while invoking God is on suicide watch, and a descent into his damaged psyche has become imperative for two women.

Appendix One

Publishing Translated Crime Fiction: The Pleasures and Pitfalls

I asked a variety of publishers what they considered to be the pleasures (and pitfalls) of publishing European crime writers in the UK in translation. I also asked if there was one book and one author that they had worked on which they found particularly gratifying.

Gary Pulsifer, Arcadia

The pleasures of publishing are multitude but it's always great to bring literature from around the world into English. Arcadia publishes writers from some 60 countries to date – and crime in translation is a fantastic vehicle to look at societal ills and interactions in particular countries. There is also the joy of recognition and discovery – and the 'ping!' of making foreign connections. I'm no different from other crime readers in hooking on to particular characters or series: Paul Johnston's Alex Mavros crime novels set in contemporary Greece are particular favourites of mine. (They are written in English but are now appearing in Greek editions.) And translated crime fiction provides an antidote to the luxury product-placement writing of the likes of Patricia Cornwell!

You ask about the pitfalls. Well... Here's an onerous one: pushing hard to establish unknown writers who can take quite some time to establish themselves in English – or, sometimes, not at all. And translations don't come cheap, even with generous subsidies.

Arcadia Euro Crime authors I've enjoyed working with include **Petros Markaris, Dominique Manotti**, winner of the International Dagger for *Lorraine Connection*, and Nicolas Freeling, who was in a sense part of the Praetorian Guard of international crime writers. Even though his fiction was written in English, his territory was very much part of that nascent EEC, covering the Netherlands, France, Belgium, Luxembourg and Germany. Who can forget the wonderful Van der Valk?

At the moment I'm finding it particularly gratifying to publish the work of the Bergen-based crime writer **Gunnar Staalesen**. His books feature private eye Varg Veum, a former social worker, and are unusual in Nordic crime for all being set in Norway's second city. Staalesen exhibits a deep understanding of human nature, not restricted to the underbelly of contemporary urban life, and it should come as no surprise that his books have sold over three million copies and have been translated into 12 languages. Indeed, in Norway there are film and TV adaptations of many of his crime novels. We have stunning new cover designs for both his front list and backlist titles and my dream is for one of the TV channels here to take up the gauntlet. He is after all, in the words of Jo Nesbo, 'Norway's Chandler'.

Patrick Janson-Smith, Blue Door

The satisfaction of publishing crime fiction in translation is derived mostly from the knowledge that one is expanding the English-speaking reader's horizons. The main danger area, especially if one has little or no grasp of languages (personally, I can manage schoolboy French, order up to ten beers and ask to be taken to the airport in German, and gesticulate wildly in Italian), is that one is reliant on the recommendations and reports of others. Other problems include the cost of translation (especially painful if one doesn't have an American partner) and the translation itself – if it isn't up to snuff, it's going to involve a lot of painstaking editorial work.

The book with which I have most enjoyed working is the Croatian-born German author **Zoran Drvenkar's** *Sorry*, a heart-stopping exploration of the darkest aspects of human nature. Very well translated by Shaun Whiteside, in my opinion it's as gripping and as chilling a thriller as Thomas Harris's *Red Dragon* or Pierre Lemaitre's more recent *Alex*. Drvenkar himself – tall, angular, a bit of a hippy (granny glasses, ponytail, a teetotaller and vegetarian), with a passion for contemporary music, film and literature, possessed of a great sense of humour – has been a pleasure to work alongside. We are preparing for the publication of his next novel, *You*, in 2014.

Maria Rejt, Mantle

I well remember the day, returning home on the Number 10 bus, when I began reading the complete translation by Stephen Sartarelli of **Andrea Camilleri's** first Inspector Montalbano novel *The Shape of Water* and was soon completely entranced. Since that journey I have published sixteen novels in the series, and in 2014, in addition to *Angelica's Smile*, the seventeenth, Mantle publishes Camilleri's *Hunting Season*, a completely captivating historical novel set in 1880s Sicily. The pleasures of publishing Andrea Camilleri are too numerous to mention (wonderful reviews, climbing sales and a very engaged readership to name but three), and the pitfalls are precisely none. Why has it taken so long for the UK market to wake up to the popularity of authors in translation? There has never been any doubt about the importance of publishing translated fiction – where would we be without Chekhov, Tolstoy and Dostoyevsky? – but now that the floodgates have opened with European authors providing the stories and characters for some of the most discussed and eagerly awaited crime series on TV it has paved the way for British publishing to catch up finally with our German, French and Scandinavian counterparts and champion literature in translation with every expectation of strong sales and significant media coverage.

So Mantle, my imprint at Macmillan, champions translated fiction on its list and for next year will include a non-European, the Korean author, **Jung-Myung Lee**, whose novel, *The Investigation*, begins with the murder of a brutal prison guard in a Japanese POW camp in 1944 and becomes an epic lament for freedom and humanity in the darkest of times; a debut crime novel, *Human Flies*, by a young Norwegian historian, **Hans Olav Lahlum**; and the concluding volume of **Håkan Nesser's** brilliant Van Veeteren cycle of novels, *The G-File*, where the retired inspector's first case also becomes his last. Perhaps the only pitfall remains that the dedicated and talented translators of such authors cannot translate quickly enough!

Ruth Tross, Mulholland Books

Working with foreign crime writers is essentially as rewarding as with good crime writers from the UK: an editor is provided with a bloody good mystery, great writing, and fantastic characters. But added to that, there is, of course, the extra pleasure of what feels a little like a holiday – a change of scene, a new culture, a variation on motives and methods and settings that are as good as a break. The other side of the coin? On a purely practical level, there's always the question of how clean a translation should be. You want to be true to the original writing – its metaphors and sentences, the atmosphere – without making it sound like it's simply been run through Google translate. So that's always a difficult balance. There's a cliché that crime in translation is easier if it's set where Brits go on holiday so they have a sense of the place already! I wonder how many people would be enticed by a novel set in the post-industrial concrete cities of Bulgaria, say... which means sometimes you have to persuade people they're interested in the country or city, though I do believe that is less of an issue these days.

Of my own authors, I am particularly proud of *The Frozen Dead* by the French author **Bernard Minier** – partly because it's the first crime in translation that I acquired, partly because I love the feeling that I am bringing a new author to a wider audience, and partly because it's just a brilliantly written book! An isolated snowbound town... an asylum for the criminally insane... a cop with a fondness for Latin tags – what else could you ask for? I'd also mention *Lonely Graves*, the first book in the Posthumus Trilogy by **Britta Bolt** (the nom-de-plume of the German Britta Bohler and the South African Rodney Bolt).

Ilaria Meliconi, Hersilia Press

The main problem for a small publisher today – in a very down to earth fashion – is, simply, money: publishers nowadays need to be genuinely remunerative if they publish for a living, not as an expensive hobby! The rise of self-publishing has also lowered (if not removed completely) the barriers to publishing. Publishers performing the function of gate-keepers has also changed. Add to that the relatively high cost of buying books (at least in paper form, and when not discounted), and it is clear why readers are therefore very wary of purchasing books by debut and translated authors. As a publisher, when you read a good review, or receive an email from someone asking when the next book in a particular series is going to appear, it is very satisfying. I am also very involved with the translation and the editing. Being an Italian speaker (we publish Italian writers), I read the books in the original, then I read the translation and sometimes discuss points with the translator, which makes me feel much more part of the process. I'm a great believer in the fact that if the translation is up to standard, a good book is a good book regardless of the language it was written in.

I really liked working on **Giorgio Scerbanenco** as he is so highly regarded in Italy – I enjoyed the feeling I was working on a classic. And I really admire his dry, sometimes cynical style: his work explores traits that are key components of human nature. It shows what an excellent observer of people he was, and what an amazing imagination he had. The historian in me thinks that I should write a book about him!

Daniela Petracco, Europa Editions

The best part of publishing crime fiction in translation in the UK is the satisfaction I get in bringing new authors, new stories, and innovative writing into a vibrant literary landscape. Translated crime novels can be viewed as cultural travel guides (complete with body count): to borrow the words of one of our authors, Brazilian writer Alberto Mussa, 'what defines a city is the history of its crimes'. At Europa Editions, our agenda is to bring to British readers books that entertain and inform, books that confront global themes through the metaphor of investigation of international crime in its local manifestations. British society is a book-loving one, and a fluid one, and little by little it is opening up to a wider range of literature from around the world. It's encouraging to see crime fiction in translation gradually leaking into the mainstream... it's already happened with a number of Scandinavian writers and I believe it will happen more frequently in future with writers from other countries.

Personally, if I have to pick titles I'm particularly proud of, then it would have to be three books; the three parts of **Jean-Claude Izzo's** *Marseilles Trilogy*. *Total Chaos*, *Chourmo* and *Solea* are exactly the kind of works that fulfil our aim, taking the reader right into the heart – and underbelly – of Marseilles, the city in Europe with the highest incidence of gun crime. Izzo writes of Marseilles' legendary organised crime scene and corrupt, violent police force, its culturally diverse society and its conflicts, but also about the sounds and smells of the city, and even the flavours of its cuisine.

Christopher MacLehose: MacLehose Press

In the field of crime fiction I do not think that taste in reading follows any group or any nationality. I believe that readers will go wherever there is exceptional quality. If there are now shelves in bookshops marked 'Scandinavian Crime' that is because we have seen an exceptional flowering of great storytelling from a relatively tiny corner of the world within three decades. **Sjöwall/Wahlöo, Peter Høeg, Henning Mankell, Karin Fossum, Arnaldur Indriðason, Jo Nesbo, Håkan Nesser, Stieg Larsson, Åsa Larsson**. These, to my mind, are the cream of the cream. They have made a remarkable contribution to the shape of present-day reading habits outside and inside Scandinavia. They have, by their sheer excellence, sown the seeds for the falling off of the very genre they represent, have made world famous. So many publishers have bought so many writers of crime novels from Scandinavian writers and sold them into translation. So many and too many. To the point that readers are already expressing disappointment. The best may be past.

We did not set out at the MacLehose Press either to turn our backs on Swedish or Icelandic crime writing or to raise a new standard elsewhere in Europe. It has, however, happened naturally that we have – from among the hundreds of noir fictions that we receive every year – found ourselves publishing a group of storytellers writing in French who are in no sense a group. They are **Antonin Varenne, Pierre Lemaitre** (who has just won the Prix Goncourt with a novel that is not a crime novel), **Hervé Le Corre, Karim Miské, Dominique Sylvain, Xavier-Marie Bonnot** and the Swiss writer **Joël Dicker**, whose novel *The Truth about the Harry Quebert Affair* was last year also shortlisted for the Prix Goncourt and has sold a few short of a million copies. Dicker's novel is not at all, nor does it set out to be, a conventional crime story. It is a crime story, but it is also a mystery and also a love story.

Such energy, such variety, such cleverness and such rich characterisation among the novels of this group. And such excellent translations too. I have always thought that a crime novelist deserved the best possible translator – such talents as Frank Wynne, Siân Reynolds, Laurie Thompson and Nick Caistor. In present-day France, for instance, is a variety of languages and vocabulary to test the very best. Anyone who watched the television crime series *Engrenage* or *Spiral* will know the sheer and wilful complexity of those voices, and will also surely have sensed that the baton was passing – before their eyes, as it were – from Scandinavian crime on television too.

Trisha Jackson, Macmillan

What I particularly enjoy about publishing crime in translation is being able to bring the sense of place and atmosphere of the cities or countryside of Europe to the page in the UK. We're extremely lucky to have authors who can not only tell a compelling crime story but also have the literary skills and talent to transport the reader to, for example, the forests, fjords and mountains of Norway; to the exciting but intimidating and grisly side of Stockholm's dark underbelly or even, although a re-imagining, Sarah Lund's bleak, but beautiful Copenhagen. The pitfalls – well I guess you have to trust a clean translation that is true and sympathetic to the original. Oh to be multi-lingual! A writer I'm proud to have brought to a UK audience in 2013 is German bestselling author, **Nele Neuhaus**. A book which has sold over 3 million copies across the world, *Snow White Must Die* became an Australian bestseller early in the year and was then selected for Richard & Judy's WHS autumn book club. The reason is quite simply that it's a page turner of epic proportions with a cast of interesting and very vividly drawn characters. But more than that it evokes life both in the city of Frankfurt and a small village in the mountainous region of the nearby Taunus. The behaviour of these small town residents offers up an interesting contrast, say, to life in a Miss Marple English village.

Robert Davidson, Sandstone Press

Our only translated crime, up to the present time, is from the Norwegian of **Jørn Lier Horst** and is his William Wisting series. So far we have published two titles: *Dregs* in 2011 and *Closed for Winter* in 2013. In 2014 we released Jørn's Glass Key and Riverton Prize winner *The Hunting Dogs* and are planning *The Caveman*. From this long term commitment it will be apparent that we have a good deal of faith in this author and the processes we have put in place, which takes us to the most obvious pitfall. Jørn Lier Horst has a great reputation across Europe but, so far, very little in the English speaking world. Therefore we are obliged to accept considerable costs to publish an author who is virtually unknown in our markets. Equally directly, we find the most obvious pleasure, which is watching him build and, I like to think, helping him. We also enjoy the pleasures of new and developing relationships and are now working not only with the author but also his translator, Anne Bruce, the Norwegian publisher, Gyldendal and, of course, NORLA (Norwegian Literature Abroad) whose support is vital.

More aesthetically, publishing Jørn Lier Horst advances our sense of internationalism and, particularly, Europeanism, by absorbing a rather different viewpoint to that of the British, Commonwealth and American public(s). Scandinavia has been marked by twentieth-century European history in ways that the native (for want of a better word) English-speaking nations have not. There has been a deeper, possibly more compromising, immersion. I think of Henning Mankell's early title *The Dogs of Riga*, where his hero, Wallander, travels to 90s Latvia, and of Jo Nesbo's *The Redbreast*, which treats the ongoing aftermath of World War Two in the Norwegian psyche. Similarly, but in his own unique way, and with the authenticity which is so much his hallmark, the mystery in Jørn's *Dregs* has its beginnings in World War Two, and *Closed for Winter* treats the post-Cold War era directly. Scandinavia and, indeed, mainland Europe are living these histories more closely than we, if these crime fictions can be taken as indicators, but the Anglophone world vibrates to the same terrible notes. These crime novels bring us a new self-identification and also serve as warnings. Of course, they are also great entertainment.

Jade Chandler, Sphere/Trapdoor/Little, Brown

Acquiring titles for a publisher of popular Scandinavian crime and thriller fiction is a pleasure. For me, one of the most gratifying things about being part of this Scandinavian fiction boom has been its effect on mainstream UK and US crime fiction readers' perceptions of what it means to read crime fiction in translation. The way that many of these readers have taken Scandinavian crime fiction to their hearts has essentially provided them with a bridge to other areas of European crime fiction and a broader and more satisfying crime-reading experience.

I have particularly enjoyed working on a novel by an award-winning French writer, **Sophie Loubière**. *The Stone Boy* (*L'enfant aux cailloux*) is an atmospheric psychological thriller with tension and suspense worthy of Hitchcock himself. The story features a wonderfully unusual protagonist, the elderly widow Madame Préau, who – on returning home from a period of convalescence – is convinced that one of her neighbour's three children is being seriously neglected, only to be told by all and sundry that said third child does not exist. This is a glimpse into a lonely, yet sharp, mind and of its owner's descent into a world of paranoia and confusion. Madame Préau's journey to discover the truth about this unloved child is utterly bewitching and takes a beautifully crafted look into what it means to be isolated whilst in the midst of your community.

For me, the beauty of crime fiction is in its universality – its comforting cycle of crime followed by punishment, or a mystery followed by a satisfying resolution. I'm delighted that I'm able to play a part in bringing page-turning, high-quality stories from around the world to English language audiences.

Julia Wisdom, HarperCollins

Many moons ago, I had a delightful Swedish editor in my office and we were discussing the blossoming of Scandinavian crime publishing in the UK. I was interested to know if she felt there were any hidden gems of authors who would do well here, and she immediately suggested **Camilla Läckberg**. For a start, while her novels were all strong on chilly psychological thrills, they also had a warm heart which readers in Sweden plainly found very engaging; each of her books had been a bestseller. And then there were the excellent central characters, Patrik Hedström and Erica Falck, the former a detective, the latter a strong, individual-minded author whom (this Swedish editor felt) female readers found especially sympathetic. I decided to take the leap and shook hands on a four-book deal over a table at the Frankfurt Book Fair. Since then Camilla has gone on to sell 14 million books worldwide, been a no. 1 bestseller across Europe, had her Hedström and Falck novels filmed for television and cinema, and been translated into 55 languages. She is particularly powerful when looking at the damage parents can wreak on their children, and how the sins of the fathers – or mothers – are handed down through the generations to cause psychological harm to families decades later. This, allied with the developing personal stories of Patrik and Erica, is a very potent combination, and highly addictive. If you throw in a wonderful sense of place – all the books are set on Sweden's beautiful eastern coast – then you can understand why Camilla's books are so popular around the world.

Sophie Buchan, Weidenfeld & Nicolson

Why go abroad for your crime scene when there are so many at home? I see the impulse towards reading translated crime as the impulse to travel. Until recently, if we wanted to peer into other nations' souls, we would do so through 'literary' novels. But few people actually did. The relative accessibility of crime fiction is opening the doors to larger numbers of tourists. As an editor, you are a tour guide of sorts, and also a first reader. To read (good) crime fiction in translation is to get in touch with the lifeblood of a country – its anxieties and paranoias, its coping mechanisms and its sense of self. Scandicrime in particular resonates because Scandinavia confuses us with its contradictions, its pristine cities set against bleak, creepy forests. Also, Scandinavian countries can give us an inferiority complex, so I think we are tickled by the idea of dark secrets among the social progress and enviable quality of life.

One of the main pleasures of publishing translated crime is the sense of discovery you feel as an editor and the fact that, if publication goes well, you will be passing that sense of discovery on to many thousands of people. It's relatively easy to buy books by UK and US authors: an agent you know sends you a manuscript and you say yea or nay. But with novels in translation, you have to follow clues. You have to track down the suspects most likely to have something of interest.

Of course there are pitfalls in publishing foreign crime but they can easily be overcome. In the same way you don't mind buying a phrase book at the airport, or having an embarrassing conversation with a waiter if the *pain au chocolat* you get at the end tastes properly *French*, you don't mind added complexities in the editing process. I edited the last few books in Russian detective novelist Boris Akunin's Fandorin series. One, *He Lover of Death*, was narrated in the first person by a nineteenth-century Muscovite street urchin. Agreeing on a translation that was both faithful to the original and comprehensible to a contemporary British audience was, of course, a challenge. But it was a fascinating challenge, and one which was entirely worth the extra effort when the positive reviews came in.

There is also the question of specificity and context. The name of a street or district or region may have particular connotations to a local audience but may just sound generically foreign to a UK reader. Of course that's problematic. But editing any novel, regardless of its language, is a negotiation between your desire to intrude (and, to your mind, improve) and your desire to stay true to the author's stated intentions. My most recent discovery is *Totenfrau* by Austrian writer, **Bernhard Aichner**, which is currently being translated by Anthea Bell. It's one of the most baroquely dark books I have ever read and also one of the most page-turning. It's a *Kill Bill* style revenge fantasy set in the chocolate-box Austrian countryside. But there are dark secrets (and cellars) and I can't wait until 2015 when we unleash this extraordinary novel onto the world. As research, the author worked as an undertaker for six months. I hope that gives you the gist.

Appendix Two

The Petrona Perspective

Since I was asked to be a judge for the first Petrona Award for Scandinavian crime fiction, I've had closer contact with three of my fellow enthusiasts for European and international crime fiction. Perhaps it was the fact that I was dotting the 'i's and crossing the 't's on the last book I did, *Nordic Noir*, that prompted the persuasive Karen Meek to get me on board. Or perhaps the fact that my multi-country Scandinavian trips to interview as many important Nordic crime writers as I could positioned me favourably in her eyes. I know she is a fan of a previous book I did on the subject, *Death in a Cold Climate*, and particularly of the latter's very translator-friendly-stance! But I was happy to take part for a variety of reasons. One was my memory of Maxine Clarke, the remarkable young woman (who wrote as 'Petrona') after whom the award was named. Maxine died far too young, and the award, leaving aside its value in recognising the best work in translated crime fiction, is a very suitable tribute. And then there was the Karen Meek factor: her work hosting the site *Euro Crime* is a notable, continuing achievement, and it provides a resource that is second to none for details, reviews and bibliographies of Scandinavian crime authors. And my other judges (apart from Karen) had equal gravitas: Sarah Ward of the authoritative *Crimepieces* and Kat Hall who writes about European crime writers for *Mrs Peabody Investigates* and specialises in German crime fiction. Between the four of us, we might modestly claim to have a finger on the pulse of Euro noir, so I asked my fellow judges which authors and books under consideration for this study had impressed them.

Karen Meek, Euro Crime (http://www.eurocrime.co.uk/)

The *Euro Crime* website has reached its tenth anniversary, and one of the main drives behind its establishment was to provide the original reading order for those authors who were being published in translation 'out of order', most notably at the time Henning Mankell. Three of my favourite European writers have also 'suffered' this fate, the Norwegians **Karin Fossum** and **Jo Nesbo** and France's **Fred Vargas**. Karin Fossum's series detective Inspector Sejer appears to varying degrees in her ten-book series and the books are never about him so it matters less what order they are read in. Her gripping English language introduction in 2002, *Don't Look Back*, the second book in the series is a more traditional crime novel than most of her other titles which tend to feature normal people trapped into doing something abnormal, and is one of my favourite books along with her *Calling Out For You*. The publishers of Jo Nesbo released book five (2005) then three (2006) in the now hugely popular Harry Hole series hoping to grip readers with an inventive serial killer plot in *The Devil's Star*, but inadvertently spoiling an emotionally shocking event in the more historically laden *The Redbreast*.

Arguably my favourite author in translation is Fred Vargas with her series featuring Paris based Commissaire Adamsberg and his collection of police detectives, all with their own unique skills. Vargas's writing is quirky beyond belief and her plots often feature seemingly otherworldly elements such as vampires or werewolves but with a rational explanation in the end. The author that most closely resembles her, I think, is Christopher Fowler with his Bryant & May series. Though I love the Commissaire Adamsberg series my favourite Vargas is *The Three Evangelists* which features a trio of three historians and an ex-policeman living in a large house with the latter having the top floor as he's 'present day' whilst the three other floors are occupied by descending time periods. The story starts with the three historians being paid to dig up a tree which has mysteriously appeared in their neighbour's front garden overnight.

Close at Vargas's heels for my favourite author is Italy's **Andrea Camilleri** who has had the luxury of being translated by the same translator (Stephen Sartarelli) *and* in the correct order *and* at a rate of two per year. To read Camilleri's irascible Sicilian Inspector Montalbano is to love him. Montalbano is a knight in this modern-day world, righting wrongs, fighting injustices but with more than an eye on a good meal and often on a beautiful woman. Camilleri recently won the CWA's International Dagger for *The Potter's Field*. Another favourite of mine in the series is *August Heat*. Though all four authors write about a policeman, their series could not be more different from each other.

Kat Hall, Mrs Peabody Investigates
(http://mrspeabodyinvestigates.wordpress.com/)

German-language crime fiction is a treasure-trove of delights, but doesn't always receive the attention it deserves in the English-speaking world. For example, how often do we hear about **Adolph Müllner's** 1828 detective story 'The Caliber', published over a decade before Poe's Dupin stories that supposedly invented the genre? Then there's the case of **Hans Fallada's** 1947 crime novel *Alone in Berlin*, a searing portrayal of the Nazi regime that was only 'discovered' by the English-speaking world when translated in 2009. Greater recognition has been accorded to the two 'fathers' of German-language crime down the years: **Friedrich Glauser**, often referred to as the 'Swiss Simenon' (although he was born in Vienna), who wrote his 'Sergeant Studer' novels in the 1930s, and Swiss author **Friedrich Dürrenmatt**, author of *The Pledge*, whose 1950s 'Inspector Bärlach' series is still greatly admired today. Both authors used the crime novel to critique society, and to probe ethical and existential questions in the turbulent years before and after the Second World War.

A number of excellent crime writers have followed in their footsteps, producing a wide range of detective novels, police procedurals, psychological thrillers, historical crime ... and, of course, German noir. Many, such as the ones below, are also available in English translation. **Petra Hammesfahr, Ingrid Noll** and **Andrea Maria Schenkel** are three outstanding contemporary German women crime writers. Hammesfahr is best known for her psychological thrillers, such as 1999's *The Sinner*, which explores the motivation for an apparently random murder, while Noll's wickedly satirical novels, such as 1994's *The Pharmacist*, dissect bourgeois, small-town life from a criminal perspective. Schenkel's *The Murder Farm* is a chilling, multi-layered exploration of a family massacre, which won the *Deutscher Krimi Preis* (German Crime Novel Prize) in 2007.

Jakob Arjouni's 'Kemal Kayankaya' series, written between 1985 and 2012, surveys Frankfurt's urban criminality through the jaundiced eyes of a Turkish-German private investigator, and uses wisecracking noir humour to challenge the stereotypes held by Germans about Turks in a clever and groundbreaking way. More recently, **Jan Costin Wagner's** 'Kimmo Joentaa' police procedurals (begun in 2003) have tapped into a melancholic Scandinavian crime tradition: set in Finland, they offer a sensitive portrayal of an investigator who solves cases while wrestling with intense personal grief.

Germany's dark twentieth-century history provides another rich area of exploration for its crime writers. **Christian von Ditfurth** and **Ferdinand von Schirach** explore the legacy of the Nazi past via investigative figures who are historians or lawyers in *A Paragon of Virtue* (2004) and *The Collini Case* (2012). Meanwhile, **Simon Urban's** *Plan D* (2011) paints a noir portrait of a 2011 Berlin in which the Wall never fell. All of these works are informed by in-depth historical research and use the crime novel as a means of presenting complex historical, legal and moral issues to their readers.

As even this very brief survey shows, German-language crime fiction is vibrant, imaginative and incredibly diverse. There's an enormous amount on offer for all crime fans to enjoy – *viel Spaß!*

(Katharina Hall is Associate Professor of German at Swansea University and runs the crime fiction blog 'Mrs. Peabody Investigates'. She is currently editing a volume entitled *Crime Fiction in German* to be published by the University of Wales Press.)

Sarah Ward, Crimepieces (http://crimepieces.com/)

Like my fellow Petrona judge Karen Meek, I think I'd pick **Fred Vargas**, revered in France for her quirky cast of characters, including the charismatic Commissaire Adamsberg. Her work has now attracted a loyal following with the exemplary English translations she's been receiving. *The Chalk Circle Man* is one of her most individual books. For more noirish writing, I'd choose **Antonin Varenne's** strongly-written *Bed of Nails*, which exposes the underbelly of Parisian society, while **Philippe Georget's** *Summertime All the Cats are Bored* honourably continues the tradition of Georges Simenon's police procedural.

Greece's social problems are ably represented by **Petros Markaris** and **Sergios Gakas**, both of whom are at pains to show how corruption in the country's elite has had a devastating effect on the lives of ordinary people. Gakas's *Ashes* is a smorgasbord of corruption and violence, while Makaris's *Che Committed Suicide* coolly documents the start of the country's problems in the run-up to the 2004 Greek Olympics.

Appendix Three

Crossing the Bridge with Sofia Helin

For the Nordic Noir magazine I edit, I interviewed the actress behind the difficult Swedish copper Saga Norén of The Bridge, *touching on its Anglo-French remake* The Tunnel...

If the obsession of British viewers for the quirky Swedish/Danish series *The Bridge* didn't quite reach the same heights as that for *The Killing*, it certainly ran *Borgen* pretty damn close – and the new season two has us energised again. The UK taste for dramatised Scandinavian crime was piqued by *The Killing*, and, to a large degree, the momentum was maintained with the later crime series. Björn Stein's *The Bridge* acquired a dedicated following, eager for the second season after its serial killer, the 'Truth Terrorist' met justice. The perfectly acceptable Anglo-French remake, *The Tunnel*, however, did nothing to slake our appetite. So what was the secret of *The Bridge*?

One crucial factor was its infuriating but likeable sociopathic heroine, Saga Norén. The series may have utilised familiar themes but it gave them an idiosyncratic twist. If you need reminding: a body is discovered on the Oresund bridge between Sweden and Denmark – two bodies, in fact, because the torso and legs belong to different victims. The ill-assorted female/male cop duo with equal jurisdiction – one Swedish, one Danish and obliged to work together on the case – are wonderfully played by Sofia Helin and Kim Bodnia.

But perfect though the amiable Bodnia was, it was the striking Sofia Helin's performance as the eccentric Saga Norén that made her a cult figure, particularly for those of us missing *The Killing*'s Sarah Lund. Sofia as Saga matched Lund's lack of interpersonal skills and pushed this to almost cosmic levels, displaying a hilarious inability to relate to other human beings. In this area, she makes even The Girl with the Dragon Tattoo, Lisbeth Salander, look as sympathetic as an agony aunt.

I knew that I had to ask Sofia about the remake of *The Bridge*, the Channel-hopping *The Tunnel*. What did she think of the actress Clémence Poésy's uncommunicative French version of Saga? Frankly, I was expecting a polite response – I couldn't see Sofia making negative remarks about another actress – but she turned the tables on me. She had seen only a short extract from *The Tunnel*, and, in the event, it was her asking me about the series. It was up to me to be diplomatic... but I began with the question she usually shakes her head at.

Barry Forshaw: I know you've been asked this before, so forgive me – but why do you think *The Bridge* has proved so popular in the UK?

Sofia Helin: The answer to that is: I don't know! And I remember that Sofie Gråbøl said something similar about *The Killing*. I have one theory about *The Bridge*: the character I play is more extreme in her behaviour than, say, Sarah Lund, so she's a kind of a phenomenon in herself. Audiences still seem to be fascinated by her, and as for the basic 'pursuit of a killer' plot – well, that's universal, and if it's well done (which I hope it is) people will be gripped by that.

BF: Isn't the most interesting thing for audiences not so much the serial killer plot as the difficult relationship between the very human Martin and the difficult, sociopathic Saga?

SH: Of course. And it goes without saying that viewers will be interested in that contrast: To some degree, Kim Bodnia's character, Martin, is there to reflect what the audience is thinking: when Saga does something outrageous or socially unacceptable, it is through his eyes that we see her – he can act as a kind of surrogate.

BF: And those interactions are often very funny...

SH: Ah ha! I think you've touched upon another reason for the success of the show. There have been brusque, blunt women detectives before – Stieg Larsson's Lisbeth Salander and Sarah Lund, of course – but, although there was dark humour there, it was sort of in the gaps and the shows were deadly serious. Although the first season of *The Bridge* dealt with the murders of homeless people, we were aware that we were making the clashes between Martin and Saga more humorous than people had seen before in such relationships – as she gets more unthinkingly rude, the audience response is amusement.

BF: Her bizarre antisocial behaviour appears to be due to a possible medical condition, but I believe that you and the writer Hans Rosenfeld never wanted to identify that as Asperger's syndrome, right?

SH: Absolutely! Audiences can draw their own conclusions as to why she behaves the way she does, but we didn't want a straightforward medical explanation that would allow audiences to pin her down and simply say: 'Ah, that's why she is the way she is.' I did study people with Asperger's syndrome, so I was able to build elements of what I'd observed into my characterisation, but this was not a kind of medical case study – that wasn't the kind of programme we were trying to make.

BF: You mention Lisbeth Salander, and, similarly, Saga in her own way does not deal with people in what most of us recognise as a 'normal' fashion – but she is different from the tattooed, hostile Lisbeth in that she does function as part of a police unit, although her colleagues regard her as odd.

SH: Yes, she is able to function with other people, even though she doesn't understand such things as the necessity to lie for the sake of people's feelings – but she can do her job, and of course she is a fantastically intuitive detective, almost (in some ways) as a result of her condition.

BF: But she remains undiagnosed...

SH: Actually, I think that the very fact that she is undiagnosed is a clue as to why the character of Saga has a certain truthfulness – and why people have accepted her. She is very intelligent, and has been able to bypass her limitations – even, perhaps, use them to do her job. It's not so much that she hasn't had time to be diagnosed, it's the fact that she doesn't feel the need – she just gets on with her life. If she needs something, she will go out and get it, although not necessarily in the most diplomatic way.

BF: As, for instance, with her sexual needs? She has an unromantic encounter in a bar, with none of the usual preliminaries and none of the necessary affection we're supposed to show after such encounters.

SH: Correct. Sex for Saga is simply an itch that needs to be scratched occasionally, with zero emotional commitment. Someone she meets in a bar will do, if he's presentable.

BF: Apart from studying people with Asperger's as you mentioned before, how did you get inside Saga's skin? Were you able to identify with her?

SH: Obviously, for an actor that is the crucial thing – you need to be able to understand why your character behaves the way they do and be... well, affectionate towards them. To like them the way you might like yourself. Initially I looked at Saga as something like a blank wall, and then something happened; that blank wall became a glass wall, and I was able to look through it and see the kind of woman she was. I was able to become Saga.

BF: As the two cities in the show are Copenhagen in Denmark and Malmö in Sweden, there is the kind of culture shock that comes when the two detectives interact; they're both Scandinavians, but to some degree are foreigners to each other. But there isn't too much about the clash of cultures in The Bridge, is there?

SH: I don't think that would be particularly interesting, do you? We obviously have to have some of that in there, and it is a Swedish/Danish co-production. We don't ignore it, but it's not necessarily a particularly interesting aspect.

BF: Kim Bodnia told me that there was more of this culture shock element in the show originally, but he persuaded people to play it down.

SH: I think we all agreed on that. The most interesting thing is the relationship between the two detectives and the tracking down of a ruthless, intelligent killer.

BF: Of course, the culture shock we've just been talking about has been transposed to another show, The Tunnel, with France and England replacing Sweden and Denmark – and Clémence Poésy playing a

French version of Saga. I don't know how many times you've already been asked this – and if you haven't, this will be the first of many – but have you seen it? And what do you think of Clémence Poésy's new version of the character you created?

SH: Please believe me that I'm not being diplomatic when I say that I can't express a view – I've only seen a short extract of it! You tell me: what's it like?

BF: Well, it's rather like the American version of *The Killing* – a perfectly creditable reimagining that nevertheless offers no real competition to the original show.

SH: Is that because you know what's going to happen in *The Tunnel*?

BF: The plot has been tweaked slightly. But Clémence Poésy is given less to do than you were, and her character is far less outlandish. But let's get back to you... do people in Sweden expect you to be like Saga when they meet you?

SH: No, they don't – I've done a lot of work over there, so people know me for a variety of things. Saga is just one of the characters I've done. That's different in England, where I'm really only known for her.

BF: I guess you'd like to change that situation?

SH: Hopefully I can! And there's a film I've made which I would hope will be shown in the UK. It's set in modern times but with a Viking theme – and if people see more of the work that I've done, they'll realise that Saga and I could not be less alike. She is light years away from the kind of personality I am. But then it's an actor's job to make you believe in the reality of a character, isn't it? And that's what I was trying to do with Saga in *The Bridge*.

Appendix Four

Jørn Lier Horst: Language – Hero – Environment

I spoke to the accomplished Norwegian author of Closed for Winter *and* The Caveman *about translated crime...*

'Translated crime – and particularly Nordic crime fiction – is everywhere. The genre's enormous impact has to be described as paradoxical: that the Nordic countries, among the most decidedly peaceful and secure places on the globe to live, have produced writers who have captivated readers the world over with their depictions of brutality and murder. I'm not the only one to wonder how that could have come about. What's the secret of Nordic Noir?

In my increasingly frequent encounters with foreign readers of crime fiction, I believe I've come closer to an answer to that enigma. Nordic crime novels are usually considered more sophisticated than, for example, American thrillers and readers comment that they have found our crime novels to be more than narratives about crime. The authors with their lofty ambitions bring a special kind of vitality and quality to the genre. Readers obviously feel a conspicuous fascination for what we might call 'Nordic melancholy', concocted from winter darkness, midnight sun, and immense, desolate landscapes. The taciturn, slightly uncommunicative Nordic crime heroes have a particular dark aura; they are lone wolves living in a barren, cold part of the world, constantly embarked on an uncompromising pursuit of truth and clarity. What's more, the entire idea of paradise lost is a prominent feature of Nordic crime: the social-democratic, efficient society attacked from within by violence, corruption and homicide.

Language – Hero – Environment

Three elements of Nordic crime fiction can be identified as crucial: the language, hero and environment.

The genre's structure of anticipated tension demands a simple, direct writing style. In Nordic crime novels, readers nevertheless find a more varied and less predictable use of language. It is true that functional, straightforward prose also dominates, but increasingly often readers come across crime novels in which the language possesses a quite obvious intrinsic value. Authors such as Karin Fossum, Håkan Nesser and Gunnar Staalesen have clearly made every effort to rise above ordinary, run-of-the-mill prose, and in their writing you find powerful literary images, condensed and convincing dialogue and linguistic sensitivity that truly enrich the reading experience.

As far as Nordic crime heroes (and heroines) are concerned, I believe they are primarily distinguished by their single-mindedness and their rebellion against authority in all its facets. The Nordic countries are egalitarian societies where, relatively speaking, there is little difference between the high and low echelons, and the social structure is far less hierarchical than in other places. Consequently our heroes, whether they are detectives, lawyers or journalists, are given the opportunity to display a certain degree of stubbornness. They can contradict their bosses at meetings, take independent decisions, and even though few in reality would go as far in their opposition as Harry Hole or Kurt Wallander, there is a strong tradition of scepticism towards authority. The integrity and sense of justice demonstrated by these heroes, combined with their human weaknesses and fantasies, shape them into people readers can identify with and want to do well.

In addition, Nordic crime novels give a great deal of space to the protagonist's private life. The reader gets to know more aspects of them than the strictly professional, and that private life naturally reflects how we live with our fellows here in the Nordic countries. Some are divorced, perhaps single parents looking after small children, and the male protagonists are considerably more equality-minded than the ones found in crime fiction from other countries. In crime series, readers can follow their heroes through different life phases as they age and alter, and the heroes are given credibility and depth as is normally demanded in characterisation within various other literary forms.

The numerous Nordic small towns presented as scenes of literary murders do not perhaps provide obvious settings for crime stories. The Nordic countries' beautiful scenery with their long coastlines, myriad skerries and snow-capped mountains inspires picturesque, enticing descriptions of nature. However, it may be that the fascination of the books lies in the very contrast between these peaceful small town communities in their attractive settings and the brutal, violent action taking place there. The narratives of Nordic crime fiction often have an unmistakable connection to their settings, and both Gunnar Staalesen's Bergen and Henning Mankell's Ystad have become magnets for tourists.

Mirror to Society

Nordic crime fiction is written by authors with a strong commitment to the losers in society, drawing attention to a social system that makes promises about protection and inclusion, but that nevertheless fails so many of its citizens. The crime novel has proved to be an excellent tool for revealing the corruption in society, greed and the misuse of power, and is therefore a very suitable instrument of social criticism. The best Nordic crime writers have a talent for creating a new political awareness in their readers. Their stories wrest us from complacent notions of our society's excellence and instead plant seeds of unease, an unease that makes it difficult to content ourselves with current conditions and that increasingly forces us to modify our view of those who turn to crime, why they do so and what motivates them. This characteristic of Nordic crime novels gives them a special earnestness, distinguishing them from other genre fiction and ensuring that their readers do not forget the book's content and import after the final page is read.

The Four Greats

The expression *Nordic Noir* is a recent one, but the Nordic method of telling crime stories is almost fifty years old. The novelists Maj Sjöwall and Per Wahlöö, with their policeman Martin Beck, created a unique genre in the mid-sixties that marked the start of a global literary fairy tale. Their books broke with the established norms of delivering pure entertainment. Social criticism and existential dilemmas were interwoven into the crime format, and the genre distanced itself from other mass-produced formula literature. The distinction between so-called 'highbrow' and 'lowbrow' forms of literature became more diffuse, and the crime novel gained admittance to the same market as other serious literary fiction.

In 1991, Henning Mankell wrote his first book about Kurt Wallander, eventually expanding this to a series of novels still making its way triumphantly around the globe. Barely a decade later, the world was introduced to Lisbeth Salander and Mikael Blomkvist through Stieg Larsson's outstanding *Millenium Trilogy*. The English edition of *The Girl with the Dragon Tattoo* sold more than 2.2 million copies in the UK, allocating it thirteenth place in the list of bestselling books ever in that country. Since then, this success has been crowned by Jo Nesbo's impressive breakthrough with millions of books sold in almost fifty countries.

Sjöwall and Wahlöö, Mankell, Larsson and Nesbo are authors who, over a long period and at various points in time, have written books of exceptional quality, thus opening the doors to Nordic crime for the rest of the world. Writers such as Arnaldur Indriðason, Håkon Nesser, Anne Holt, Gunnar Staalesen, Karin Fossum, Jussi Adler-Olsen and Liza Marklund have followed in their footsteps and are numbered among those who have put the Nordic countries well and truly on the literary map.

Film and TV

Further to this, a number of dark Danish TV series have opened the eyes of an international audience to Nordic crime. In 2007, the Danes rolled out twenty episodes of *The Killing*, a high-quality, well-crafted production that grabbed attention. When the first episode was broadcast on British television, it attracted more than 400,000 viewers. The Danish-Swedish co-production, *The Bridge*, also became extremely popular. Both series led to the making of English language equivalents, and the same happened when the BBC made a television series about Kurt Wallander and, in 2011, when Stieg Larsson's book *The Girl who Played with Fire* appeared as an American film version. This insight into the Nordic crime world has increased the love of reading. Success on TV and cinema screen has produced a growing demand for Nordic crime literature. Yesterday an Indian literary critic told me that Bollywood is about to film a remake of *The Killing* in Hindi. Russian and Turkish film companies apparently also have similar plans.

The Answer

Viewed in their totality, Nordic crime novels are extremely varied when it comes to description of landscape, characters, language, plot and action. All the same, they are obviously regarded as relatively uniform by readers in other parts of the world. And of course, as a region, we do share a common history and tradition, and have several external features in common as far as social structure, welfare, political system and values are concerned.

As previously mentioned, both psychological and sociological explanations can be found as to why Nordic crime fiction has made such a powerful international impact, but we also know that readers and publishers abroad have, throughout the past fifty years, been gradually introduced to this method of storytelling. Many different participants have contributed to this phenomenon: authors, publishers, literary agents, critics, enthusiasts and an enormous marketing apparatus have worked together to create increased interest in crime literature from the Nordic countries, ensuring that *Nordic Noir* has become an expression not only widely recognised but also one with real resonance. However, everyone who works with books is aware that enthusiasm and generous marketing budgets do not in themselves create the big bestsellers. In order for a book to become a worldwide phenomenon, something else has to happen: each and every individual reader has to become passionate about it. They have to recommend the book to their aunt, their neighbour, and their workmate. And in order for that to happen, the reading experience has to be more than sheer entertainment. This is where I believe that Nordic crime is exceptional. At its best, the novels possess the ability to imitate real life with originality and elegance, with linguistic precision and psychological depth. They are full of ghastly crimes and protracted tension, yet simultaneously contain a profound yearning. The yearning for a lost paradise, for *"folkhemmet"* or the people's home, for the vision of a welfare state, all of which are increasingly threatened by powerful new forces.

Jørn Lier Horst (translated by Anne Bruce) 19/1/2014.

Appendix Five

SELECTED TOP CRIME NOVELS BY COUNTRY

ITALY
Carlo Emilio Gadda *That Awful Mess on the Via Meruluna*
Umberto Eco *The Name of the Rose*
Andrea Camilleri *The Wings of the Sphinx*
Leonardo Sciascia *The Day of the Owl*
Gianrico Carofiglio *Temporary Perfections*
Carlo Lucarelli *Carte Blanche*
Luigi Guicciardi *Inspector Cataldo's Criminal Summer*
Giancarlo De Cataldo *Romanzo criminale*

FRANCE
Emile Zola *Thérèse Raquin*
Georges Simenon *The Man Who Watched Trains Go By*
Boileau & Narcejac *Les diaboliques/The Fiends*
Dominique Manotti *Rough Trade*
Fred Vargas *Wash This Blood Clean from My Hand*
Pierre Lemaitre *Alex*
Jean-Claude Izzo *The Marseilles Trilogy*

GERMANY
Friedrich Dürrenmatt *The Pledge*
Simon Urban *Plan D*
Jan Costin Wagner *Silence*
Hans Fallada *Alone In Berlin*
Jakob Arjouni *Happy Birthday, Turk!*
Paulus Hochgatterer *The Mattress House*
Ferdinand von Schirach *The Collini Case*

SPAIN & PORTUGAL
Manuel Vázquez Montalbán *Murder in the Central Committee*
Domingo Villar *Water-Blue Eyes*
Eugenio Fuentes *At Close Quarters*
Luis Fernando Verissimo *The Spies*
Antonio Hill *The Summer of Dead Toys*
Arturo Pérez-Reverte *The Dumas Club*
Teresa Solana *The Sound of One Hand Killing*

GREECE
Yannis Maris *The Man on the Train*
Alexis Stamatis *Bar Flaubert*
Petros Markaris *Che Committed Suicide*
Ioanna Bourazopoulou *What Lot's Wife Saw*
Andreas Apostolides *Lobotomy*

THE NETHERLANDS
Maarten 't Hart *The Sundial*
René Appel *The Third Person*
A.C. Baantjer *Murder in Amsterdam*
Saskia Noort *The Dinner Club*
Simone Van Der Vlugt *Safe as Houses*
Charles den Tex *Chance in Hell*

POLAND
Marek Krajewski *The End of the World in Breslau*
Zygmunt Miloszewski *Entanglement*

ROMANIA
George Arion *Attack in the Library*
Bogdan Hrib *Kill the General*
Oana Stoica-Mujea *Anatomical Clues*

THE SCANDINAVIAN COUNTRIES
Maj Sjöwall & Per Wahlöö *The Laughing Policeman*
Peter Høeg *Miss Smilla's Feeling for Snow*
Henning Mankell *The Faceless Killers*
Arnaldur Indriðason *Jar City*
Yrsa Sigurðardóttir *Last Rituals*

Håkan Nesser *The Strangler's Honeymoon*
Jussi Adler-Olsen *Mercy*
Gunnar Staalesen *Cold Hearts*
Camilla Läckberg *The Lost Boy*
Jo Nesbo *The Redbreast*

Appendix Six

SELECTED TOP CRIME FILMS & TV PER COUNTRY

ITALY

Salvatore Giuliano (Film, 1962, Francesco Rosi, director)
Investigation of a Citizen Above Suspicion (Film, 1970, Elio Petri, director)
The Conformist (Film, 1970, Bernardo Bertolucci, director)
The Mattei Case (Film, 1972, Francesco Rosi, director)
Lucky Luciano (Film, 1973, Francesco Rosi, director)
Inspector Montalbano (TV, 1999–, various directors)
Romanzo criminale (Film/TV series, 2005, Michele Placido et al, directors)
Gomorrah (Film, 2008, Matteo Garrone, director)

FRANCE

Pépé le Moko (Film, 1937, Julien Duvivier, director)
Touchez pas au grisbi/Hands off the Loot! (Film, 1954, Jacques Becker, director)
Les diaboliques/The Fiends (Film, 1954, Henri-Georges Clouzot, director)
Rififi/Du Rififi chez les hommes (Film, 1955, Jules Dassin, director)
Classe tous risques/Consider All Risks (Film, 1960, Claude Sautet, director)
Le cercle rouge (Film, 1970, Jean-Pierre Melville, director)
Engrenages/Spiral (TV, 2005–, Philippe Triboit, Pascal Chaumiel et al, directors)
Caché/Hidden (Film, 2005, Michael Haneke, director)
State Affairs (Film, 2009, Éric Valette, director)
Braquo (TV, 2009, Olivier Marchal, director)

GERMANY
M (Film, 1931, Fritz Lang, director)
The Testament of Dr Mabuse (Film, 1933, Fritz Lang, director)
Run, Lola, Run (Film, 1999, Tom Tykwer, director)
The Lives of Others (Film, 2006, Florian Henckel von Donnersmarck, director)
The Silence (Film, 2010, Baran bo Odar, director)

SPAIN & PORTUGAL
Black God, White Devil (Film, 1964, Glauber Rocha, director)
The Crack (Film, 1981, José Luis Garcia, director)
Call Girl (Film, 2007, António-Pedro Vasconcelos, director)

THE SCANDINAVIAN COUNTRIES
Wallander (TV, 2005–2012, various directors)
Jar City (Film, 2006, Baltasar Kormákur, director)
Van Veeteren (TV, 2000–2006, various directors)
The Killing (TV, 2007–2012, various directors)
Easy Money (Film, 2010, Daniel Espinosa, director)
False Trail (Film, 2011, Kjell Sundvall, director)
The Bridge (TV, 2011–, various directors)
The Hour of the Lynx (Film, 2013, Søren Kragh-Jacobsen, director)

Index

Index